PHOTOSHOP AND ILLUSTRATOR

SEAN DONOHUE
JEMMA GURA
NICK HIGGINS
ADRIAN LUNA

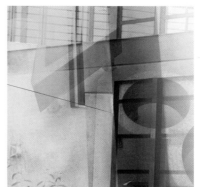
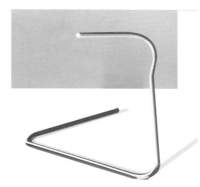
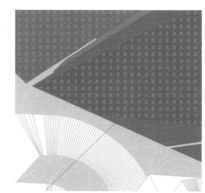

friendsof

DESIGNER TO DESIGNER™

4X4 LIGHT & DARK

PHOTOSHOP AND ILLUSTRATOR

Trademark Acknowledgements

First printed November 2001

Published by friends of ED Ltd. 30 Lincoln Road, Olton, Birmingham. B27 6PA
Printed in USA
ISBN 1903450454

PHOTOSHOP AND ILLUSTRATOR

4X4 LIGHT & DARK

credits

authors
sean donohue
jemma gura
nick higgins
adrian luna

author agent
mel jehs
gaynor riopdre

project administrator
fionnuala meacher

copyright research
fionnuala meacher

team leader
mel orgee

index
simon collins
emily colborne

cd
tom bartlett

content architect
catherine o'flynn

lead editor
jim hannah

editors
julie closs
richard o'donnell
ben renow-clarke

graphic editor
katy freer

technical reviewers
janine badger
corné van dooren
andrés yánez durán
vicki loader
jeroen meeuwissen
todd simon

technical consultants
peter aylward
kristian besley

creative consultant
sunny ralph
www.freshfroot.com

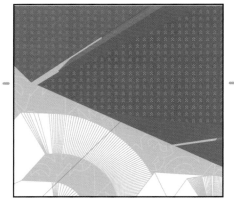

JEMMA GURA: 1

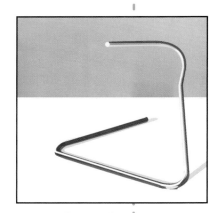

NICK HIGGINS: SS

ADRIAN LUNA: 111

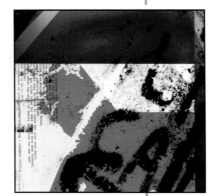

SEAN DONOHUE: 165

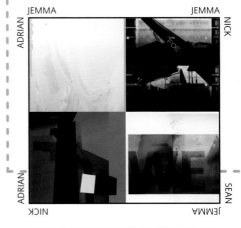

NOISE AND INTERFERENCE 219

photograh courtesy of Manuel Tan

SEAN DONOHUE

Sean Donohue, 26, grew up in Yonkers, New York, where he spent most of his youth and teenage years in ice hockey rinks slapping around 8oz of vulcanized rubber. He attended School of Visual Arts in NYC for a year and graduated from The State University of New York at Oswego in Oswego, NY in 1997.

Now hailing from the Sunnyside section of Queens, NYC, he's currently working as senior designer for Brooklyn based HUGEinc. When time, energy, and ideas permit, Sean works on his personal/journal site, goingonsix.com.

Goingonsix.com was a finalist at Flash Forward NYC's 2001 Flash Film Festival in the Motion Graphics category and select works from the site will be appearing in the upcoming book titled '72-dpi: Anime' by Die Gestalten Verlag.

JEMMA GURA

Trained as a fine artist, Jemma made her exodus into web at the advent of MOSAIC. Her duties include keeping Prate.tm [prate.com] on brand, managing regular updates and answering questions about the Prate Open Source.tm files.

She maintains executive level.02 status in MEGACORP.tm, the aggressive ultra-capitalist twilight corporation of unknown origin. The affiliations between MEGACORP.tm and H-CORPS.tm [h-corps.com] remain unconfirmed, but public access to the (one)CYCLE.OCCUR [onecycleoccur.com] project exist sporadically.

Her work has been in a couple books & magazines... here and there... and she should probably start sending copies to her parents.

NICK HIGGINS

Started 1960, Devon, England. Attended a freaky school until age 11. Left before it got really freaky.Ordinary school until 18. After which, Manchester University, Geography Degree. Developed an interest in photography. Left Manchester 1981, just before the Hacienda opened. Geography is now very unfashionable, but it had great diagrams and pictures in all of the text books. I moved to London in 1981, worked in a bottom-feeding area of music retail. During this employment, I started a foundation art course, expecting to go into photography or graphics. Unexpectedly, I left the course concentrating on drawing. Went on to Central St.Martins, leaving as an illustrator. Since then I have worked as an illustrator, for various people. Parallel to commercial commissions I have produced a lot of paintings, photography, books and pamphlets, embroidery and other things.

ADRIAN LUNA

I have been searching for my edge for many years, and have endeavored upon many creative theories and methods that have become a base formula for my designs. By day I am a designer working with freelance clients on projects ranging from Flash animation engines to creative high-res imagery. By night I am a new media artist. I have five years' user interface experience with such clients as Adidas, Sempra Energy, Home Depot, Farmers Insurance, Beckton Dickinson, Duke University Medical Center, and William Morris Agency. I was recently the Creative Director for Digital Evolution (formerly US Interactive), but have just moved to freelance. This in turn opened the door to a lazy beach bum lifestyle and offers genuine thinking time. I love it!

The 4

The four authors of this book seem to have little in common. Read through the theory sections, look at the artworks: they are poles apart. But there are certain lines of longitude that connect them:

- a visual style that is distinctive, innovative and influential
- a hunger for the experimental and a tendency to take risks
- a wealth of experience and a firm control of the tools they use

We were excited by their work, we wanted to see how they would approach the same theme, we knew they would have a lot to say and even more to show.

The 4x4

Most books are fossils. Designers look back on their body of work, they discuss pieces they once created in response to motivations they once had. We sit on the outside and gaze in at the pinned exhibits.

This book is not a spectator and it is not a museum piece. The 4x4 Project is a catalyst and the authors words, the readers thoughts, the artworks and the theories are all ongoing reactions in the creative process.

This book is a laboratory where you can learn from and participate in experimentation.

The accompanying CD provides you with relevant source files for the tutorials, the final, exclusive artworks in unflattened PSD format and all remixes and digital hybrids spawned by the Project....the next step is yours.

enter the 4x4 project

phase 1 - the book in your hand
phase 2 - the experiment continues online

you have the theme
you have the source files
respond
react
create
combine

file-swap with other readers
create hybrids with the artists' works
share inspirations
innovate, experiment

www.friendsofed.com/4x4

The Penkiln Burn is a small river in the southwest of Scotland. It rises in the Galloway Hills at the Nick of Curleywee. It tumbles and turns for eight and a half miles, passing on the way Sheuchan Craig, Lamachan, Glen Shallock, Auchenleck, Garlies Castles and Cumloden before it flows into the River Cree at the village of Minnigaff.

Bill Drummond (www.penkiln-burn.com)

At least that's what Drummond says. I don't particularly care if it is true or not.

Create your own myth. Develop a set of rules and standards that amuse you... then build a body of work with proper documentation following that structure. Be prepared and willing to take it all the way... no holds barred. If this seems irrelevant or absurd, proceed to the nearest body of fresh water during a full moon. Bring with you one stone, painted #EA3B1E, weighing no more or less than 45 grams, and your hard-drive. Toss your drive into the water and leave the stone on the shore as a marker.

I want tomorrow today. I'm looking for the new cosmetic reality. And I'll be doing this till I die. Every time I find something that looks or sounds new, I feel like I'm riding a high for a few days. Then I crash. I fall much harder after stumbling across something new in my own work – I suppose it's the pride that does it? I miss the future. There's nothing like it. I wish people would stop being content in this standard aesthetic in visual design. It's boring me to tears.

I fly Air Kazakhstan.

When Mosaic was released, I stopped painting. What was the point of it anymore, we were on the cusp of a new horizon. Lives were to be changed, drastically. New protocols had to be developed. Metaphors of old media weren't going to port over. Oh, I didn't know all that back then. All I saw was something new, and that was good enough.

I certainly didn't see 'design' – that came later.

747

X X X X X X X
X X X X
X X X X X X X

My grandfather, Jules Laroche, came from a family that raised horses in Lac Megantic, Canada. The Laroche family is notorious for being full of pranksters. Jules was the youngest of all the brothers and had severe problems sleeping due to booby-traps and such like. He was sent to live with his grandmother at an early age, because his parents were worried about him being tormented by his ruthless brothers and their practical jokes.

It's every man for himself at my parent's house during visits from my grandfather's brothers. In my lifetime, I've seen smoke bombs go off in the kitchen and lawn sprinklers turn on while people are sunbathing. These are old men. I surely missed out on some better pranks when they were younger.

When Jules grew up, he traded papers with an American guy named Leo, so Leo could work in Canada and Jules could work in the States. So when 'Leo' was drafted into the US Army during the tail-end of WW2, my grandfather went to Berlin under his assumed identity and rebuilt German bridges after the war. When his tour of duty came to an end, he revealed himself to the proper authorities as an imposter. The US Government, pleased that a foreigner served for our country, offered him citizenship, but my grandfather refused and instead requested only to live in the US permanently. Request granted.

I should pay some hipster NYU student living in Williamsburg to write this for me.

Jules Laroche + family.

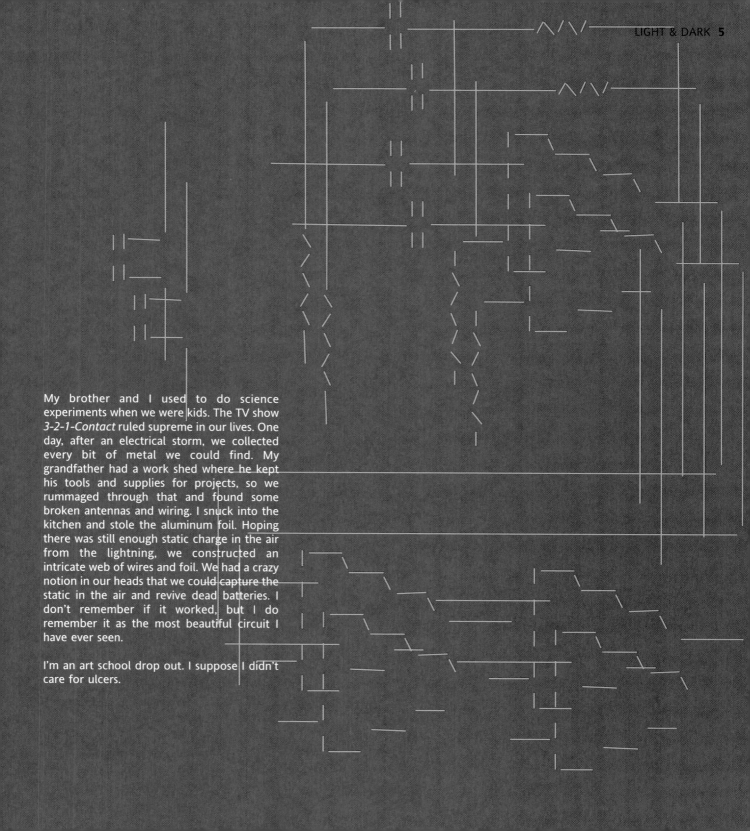

My brother and I used to do science experiments when we were kids. The TV show *3-2-1-Contact* ruled supreme in our lives. One day, after an electrical storm, we collected every bit of metal we could find. My grandfather had a work shed where he kept his tools and supplies for projects, so we rummaged through that and found some broken antennas and wiring. I snuck into the kitchen and stole the aluminum foil. Hoping there was still enough static charge in the air from the lightning, we constructed an intricate web of wires and foil. We had a crazy notion in our heads that we could capture the static in the air and revive dead batteries. I don't remember if it worked, but I do remember it as the most beautiful circuit I have ever seen.

I'm an art school drop out. I suppose I didn't care for ulcers.

I've been collecting Spawn toys since the early 90s, they are made by some crazy dude named Todd McFarlane. I have a couple of things that I look for when choosing new additions to my collection, but there is one major test. I hold the toy above my head and imagine what it would be like waking up to it, hovering there, in the middle of the night. If I think it will make my heart stop, I buy it. There are a lot of people collecting Spawn and plenty of *ebay* junkies and commerce sites surrounding these toys. But most people never play with their collection. They just buy the toys and keep them in their boxes. I've never quite understood that. Don't they remember what it was like being a kid and having toys your mom didn't want you to play with because you might break them or hurt yourself or whatever? It was pure torture! People are weird.

So I get this big box at the office a couple months ago and I open it up to find that Mike Cina had sent me the über-Spawn toy. It is six separate action figures that connect into one HUGE spawn monster. It was sort of a bribe to get me to move to Minneapolis, which will happen... someday soon. The thing is, it doesn't come put together. You have to do this yourself. It took me almost two hours, but I still have pieces left over and I can't figure out where they go. The only other person I know who has this Spawn is Manny Tan of uncontrol.com. Maybe he will read this and feel bad enough for me to come over and finish it. Manny sent me photos of his toy, fully constructed. Maybe I should just use his photos as a diagram and stop being so lazy.

Track 5 rock eternal.

I have a secret hobby. I follow fashion. Oh, don't get me wrong, I dress for like crap for the most part. Yes, yes, it's mostly because I can't afford Comme des Garcons - but I know people who make less than I do and manage to pull off a couple of trips to Century 21, some sample sales and make it work. I don't like to shop. I love new clothes, but the actual act of shopping I hate. It's always such a mission! I just don't have the dexterity for pushing through the crowds in Soho, then rummaging through racks and racks with women who settled for a millionaire husband and a nice Celine handbag. It's depressing.

So anyway, if I could choose one and only one designer to dress me, I would wear Comme des Garcons. The house is headed up by a Japanese woman named Rei Kawakubo. She rocks. If any person has been influential in red being my color of choice, it's her. She in fact once said, "Red is the new color black". Of course, that was many seasons ago... but I can't let go of the color red. It is perfection of the visual spectrum incarnate.

Did you know that I can get frozen strawberry margaritas delivered to my apartment? Brooklyn isn't always that bad.

Hussein Chalayan graduated from St. Martins in 1993. That year, *The Face* did an article showcasing some of the best talent graduating with pieces from their senior collections. I saw Hussein's work and immediately took note, raving about him to my friend Alejandro Perez, a fashion photographer in Miami. The next year, Hussein presented his first solo collection which was quite a success, as he has in each successive year. He was voted British Fashion Designer of the Year for 2000, and as the critical acclaim grows, so does my pride. I think back to his collection from school and remember with glee that I was the first in my circle of 'fashion-industry' friends to take notice. I think it was my best moment of forethought.

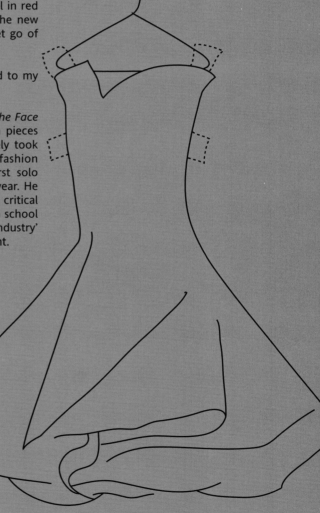

I never liked Gianni Versace. I loathed him, actually. Maybe because I never forgot the sickening way he dressed women in the 80s: leopard-print spandex and gold lame galore. It was vile. In the early 90s when I lived in Miami he bought an apartment building on South Beach, and kicked everyone who lived there out. He then converted it to his own little mini-mansion. The really gross thing was that is was smack-dab on Ocean Drive, the busiest strip in Sobe, with full-on tourist action. How bourgeois is that? After a year of boasting that someday I would throw a raw steak onto his front door my friends made me do it. OK, they didn't force me, but I'm sure they got sick of my rambling and figured this would get it out of my system.

I walked up Gianni's steps with a freshly bought, bloody steak, pulled it out of the plastic coverings and swung it, with all my might, at his front-door. While my friends were taking photos (because who would ever believe it without photographic evidence) two security monkeys, dressed in those obscene Versace-print satin shirts, approached. They were real slow in the membrane. One grabbed my arm, and the other said to him, "Stop. You can't touch her". They were in shock, not quite sure what to do when they were only trained to protect the house from mobs of poorly-dressed fans. They were confused, I knew it, and I wasn't going to wait around while their synapses caught up. I simply walked away, with the two guards standing on the steps, trying to remember their names.

The next year I was working in San Francisco for Young & Rubicam, designing banners for Novell, when it happened. Gianni was shot and killed on those very steps, by Andrew Cunanan. You can believe I got a couple phone calls at the office that morning from friends, making sure I had an alibi.

Life will become boring and petty if you lend too much importance to your own boring and petty struggles.

Damian Stephens is an English transplant, in Cape Town, South Africa. He is currently the Creative Director for the Type01 studio (*www.type01.com*) and Dplanet (*www.dplanet.org*). Although he refuses to call himself a mere designer, he is one of the few people I have met with groundbreaking thought and a solid grasp on interactive media. He's brilliant. If you ever run into him, call him an art-fag. If he is about to do some kung-fu action on you, just defend yourself by saying I told you to say it. Hopefully, enough people will have called him art-fag that he will eventually become numb and accept it.

Every aspect of life needs to be approached as an exceptional situation. Otherwise, you won't grow from that experience... and maybe you should think about paying someone else to do your laundry.

Mr. Smith was an English teacher I had in high school. He was from Wales. I don't really know what that means, being an American and thinking all English are English, but what I do know is he was cool-as-moo. He's one of those teachers that people easily remember twenty years after being in his class. I doubt all of them remember him fondly, but those who had problems were probably dumbasses. Mr. Smith didn't take kindly to those with poor cognitive responses. You didn't have to be the best student, you didn't have to do your homework, as long as you were of good character and could think for yourself, you were golden.

Mr. Smith once told me I wrote like I had a stick up my butt, and I know why...

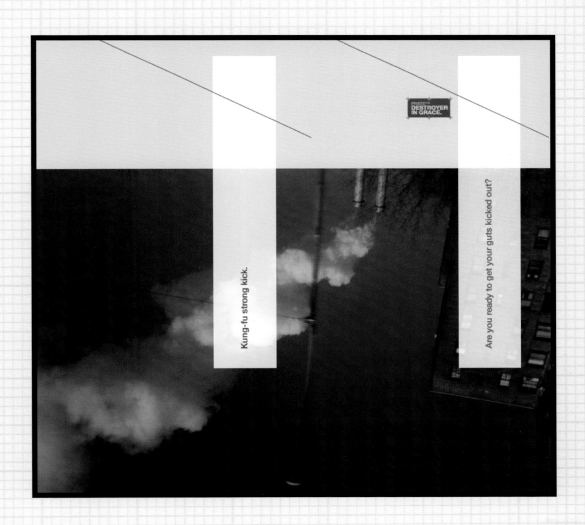

After trying to conform to the structure of school a few years earlier, I realized the key was understanding 'the formula'. I had absorbed enough slack in other classes for asking good yet 'peculiar' questions. There is a formula to writing papers in school. In fact, there is a formula for everything in high school, from passing algebra tests to sitting at the 'cool kids' lunch table. I understood, lived and loved the formula. I wrote all my papers in that tried and true manner resulting in each one sounding like a mutual fund prospectus. And hell, that was good enough for me, because it wasn't some hippie 'creative writing' class I was trying to pass. God knows I have no tolerance for poetry. Mr. Smith had no tolerance for mutual fund prospectus-styled writing.

He was a serious coffee drinker, sporting his own personal coffee maker in the back of the class. He also had a coffee mug he kept on his desk, with a plastic roach in it. He never washed his mug. Now I never understood the reasoning behind this, but I knew it must have been important to him. It was a well-known fact that Mr. Smith was simply not down with having a clean coffee mug.

One day the class clown washed his mug. He was one of those kids that weren't very smart and people kind of made fun of him. I think his sophomoric jokes were just one of those failed attempts to get people to like him... you know the type. So he washed Mr. Smith's coffee mug. I've never seen Mr. Smith flip out like that. The kid was kicked out of his class. Permanently.

Mr. Smith made his own set of rules and standards; he chose how the environment would revolve around him. If that meant having a coffee mug with a plastic roach in it that he never washed, then he lived and died by that. It didn't matter that nobody else understood the rules and standards. Only that Mr. Smith was prepared to take it all the way.

He passed me with honors – he was one cool mother. And I'll never forget the coffee mug.

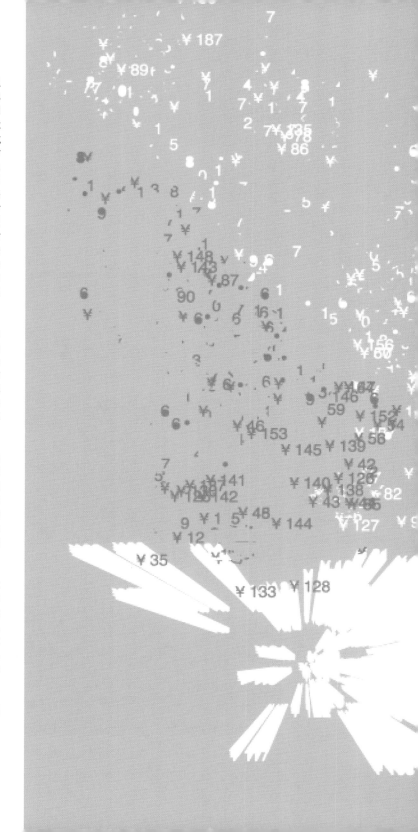

The catalyst for most of what I do, aside from client work, is amusement. I have ideas, just like everyone else, like putting photos up on *www.prate.com*, or taking some Illustrator files that Mike Cina and I have passed back and forth and posting them, putting up some news that may be important to me, but I filter most of this out. It's when an idea that I really feel is funny or amusing or even just new to me pops into my head, that I go ahead and start posting.

I like concepts that get me thinking. Concepts that can be built on and have futures are the ones I try to roll with. Something you can take all the way. Something you can spend long periods of time on, adding to it, evolving it. It isn't necessarily going to be evident to a viewer at my site. It could exist entirely in my process, and quite often does. I'm not as driven by the self-publishing aspects of the web, as I am by the promise of keeping me occupied and amused. Communicating ideas or messages to those visiting Prate is not in my mission statement and is entirely off-brand for Prate. There is no narrative, no story, no agenda. An implied attitude, maybe.

I've gotten a lot of inspiration from Ed Ruscha. He's one of those fine artists like Jenny Holzer where his work is somewhat designerly and overly-stylized. But his work is fantastic! Brilliant – really. He takes these canvases and on a simple, minimal backdrop paints phrases or single words: "*they called her styrene*", "*keychain music*", "*those of us who have double-parked*". They go on and on, hundreds and hundreds of these paintings. Sometimes he will vary the use of his fonts, or the atmosphere where the words will float, but the concept is the same. He's been doing the same thing for years. Taking it all the way.

I have a photo of Ed Ruscha framed in my bedroom. He is sitting on a chair reading a book entitled – *Mean as Hell*. I really love that photo.

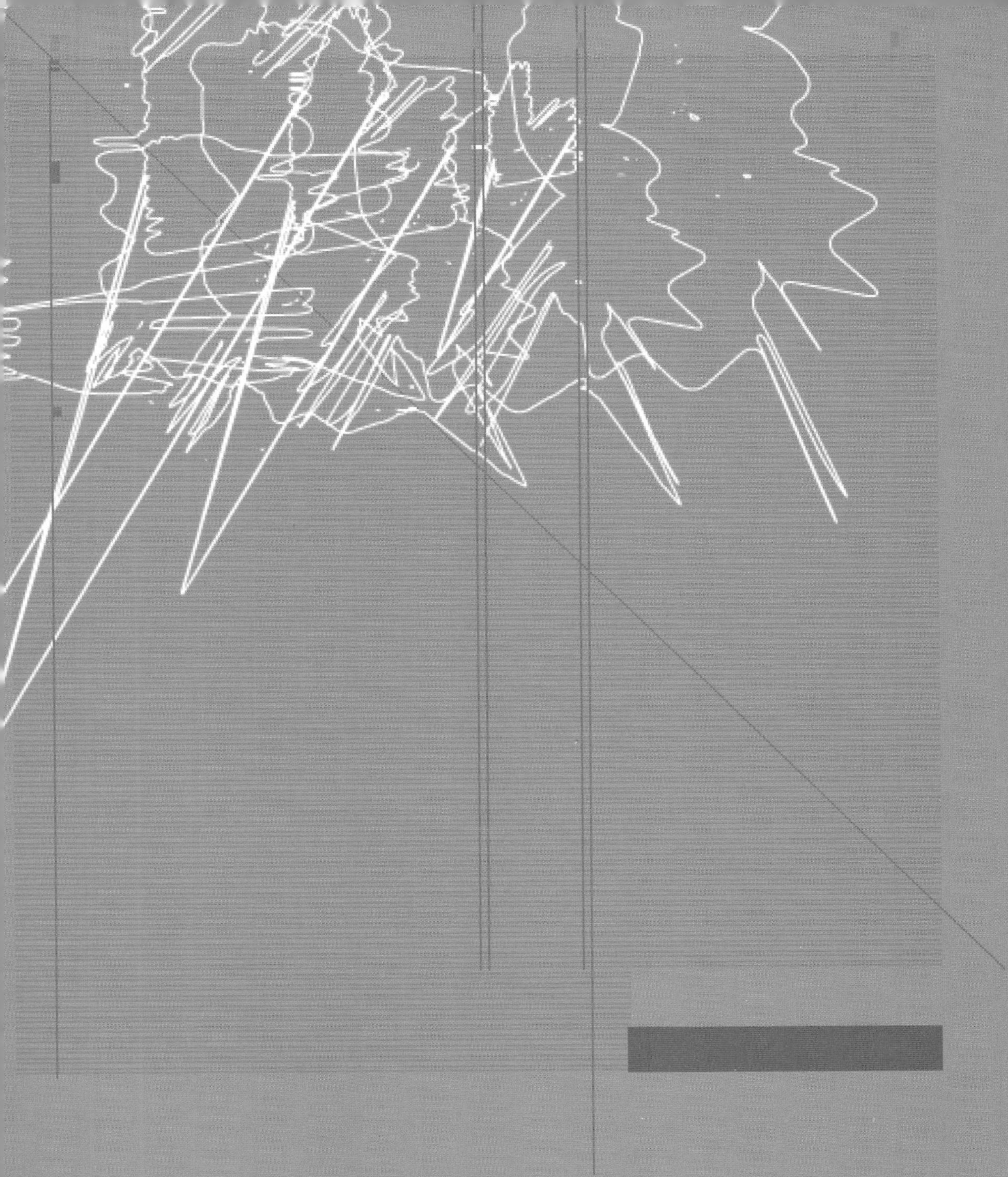

I enjoy using one method, repeating it over and over again on a single file. In Illustrator, you don't have to worry about the artifacting and quality loss you would soon end up with when running a filter repeatedly on the same file in Photoshop. Taking one idea all the way.

In my piece for this book, I started out with the words *Light & Dark*. Next, I decided on a method. Then, all I did was repeat, repeat and repeat. One continuous rhythm until I was satisfied that I had taken it as far as the consensus of aesthetics would allow. Have I mentioned taking one idea as far as you can? I'm sick of reading it myself. Let's talk about something else.

I just found out that in the area where my father's family is from, they spell my last name with one of those u's with the two dots on top of it. Now I have to picture my name completely differently.

This tutorial charts the progression of a piece from its beginnings in Illustrator through to its completion in Photoshop. On the way I'll enlist the assistance of a couple of plug-ins and extras. In the process of creating the final piece I'll build up a collection of Illustrator designs, and then select from them the themes and files I think will work well when bundled together into the final Photoshop composition.

The main plug-in I'll be utilizing comes from Kai Software. It's a plug-in for Adobe Illustrator 8 called Kai's Power Tools (KPT) Vector Effects. Although it is a plug-in, it's not really my style to do the civilized thing and point-and-shoot with it. I think it's important to wrestle full-on with these things, otherwise you risk producing lifeless and boring results.

You have to bend filters, push them to their limits, and tweak them out in order to get something new. I'll be looking at how this may be achieved - and I'll give you a hint right now about what I'm thinking: it may be beneficial to have a computer without top of the range processing speeds.

Of course, even pushing the boundaries can get a bit predictable after a while, and as much material is going to hit the ground as takes off, but at least this way there's always the chance of something completely unexpected happening. That is what I try to end up with: something unforeseen and awkward.

With this in mind, the following section outlines how I arrived at my final composition, having started out using text as the medium.

There is a degree of randomness in the exact creation of the composition, but the techniques used are not. They are there to enable you to experiment and create an original composition.

Image 1: pushing the perspective

Okay, so let's face the blank screen for as short a time as possible. After creating a new Illustrator document, I typed out the words '4x4 Light & Dark' in a typeface that Photoshop master Mike Cina created. I then converted the type to outlines via the Type drop-down menu.

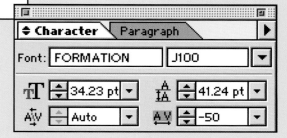

Next, I opened KPT Vector Effects and ran a 3D Transform filter, pushing the perspective and extrusion values to the max.

This filter leaves you with three major parts to the image:

- The original vector shapes at the front

- A smaller, skewed mirror of the original vector shapes at the back

- The complex perspective-driven piece that connects the front to the back parts, achieving the 3D quality.

After setting up the filter I chose to go with random variables for rotate on all three axes (x, y, z), and coupled them with the axis origin option until I got lovely red letters in the preview screen saying "Some objects are behind the viewer. Try decreasing the perspective".

This is the point at which a reasonable person would stop and reset the variables in order to pacify their computer and get rid of the "error". That's when I run the filter because, well, where's the fun in being reasonable?

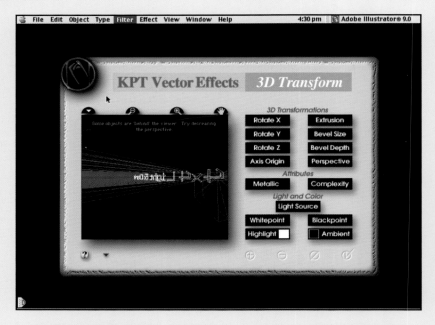

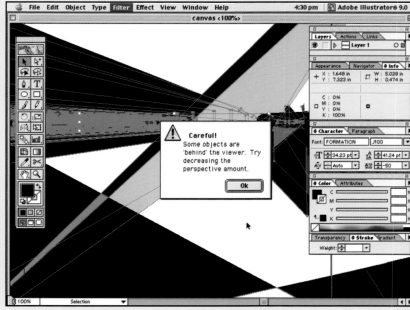

At first glance what we are presented with here is a huge mess. To cope with this I'll select all (CMD A / CTRL A) and then shrink by 50% or more in order to view all of the results on the canvas. All of the pieces at this stage will be grouped together, and can be ungrouped by selecting all and pressing CMD+SHIFT+G on a mac, or CTRL+SHIFT+G on a PC. This allows me to move or manipulate individual pieces of the picture at will, so having played around with the style and architecture of the piece until I become bored of looking at it, I'll save the piece and open a new document.

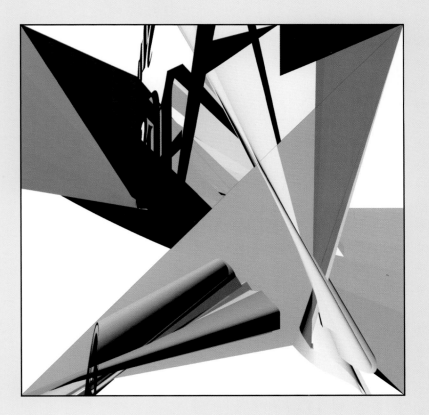

Image 2: Stack 'em high

Now I'll repeat the same 'technique' on the words 'lightanddark' in Helvetica, stacked four-high.

Here I'll choose random variables for the axes, with perspective set to the maximum. To try and exercise a certain aspect of control in the results I can utilize the undo and redo functions, while altering the variable values, until I reach a result I'm happy with.

One of these trials lead to the words being stacked, moving up at an angle, with the bottom left side cut off by the edge of the canvas, and a single line sticking out of it at 45 degrees, as you can see in the diagram below.

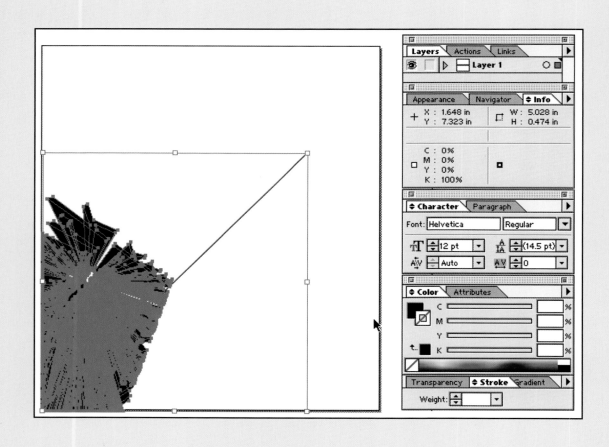

You may be able to see that, despite their altogether different appearance, certain remnants of the words and letters are still intact and legible.

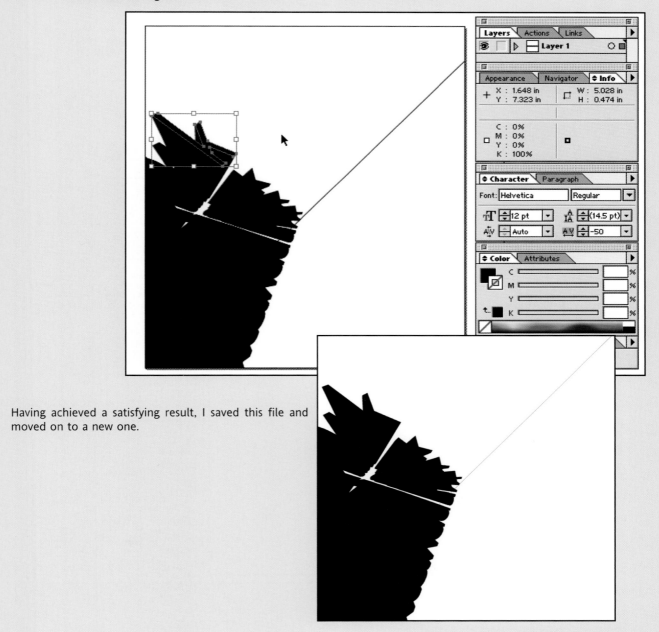

Having achieved a satisfying result, I saved this file and moved on to a new one.

Image 3: Let's give that another go

The last result made me curious enough to repeat the same variables (CMD E / CTRL E will run Apply Last Filter remembering the settings you last used) on exactly the same words, stacked four-high, but using the Teutonic-looking font named Fette Fraktur instead of plain old Helvetica.

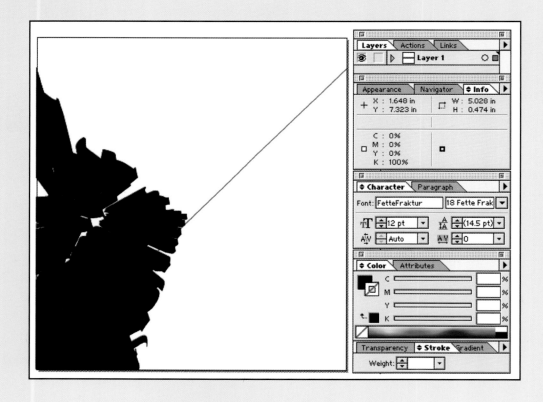

If you compare this with the previous Helvetica result, the curves of this black-faced font are a shade more interesting. So, happy enough, I cleaned up some stray shapes, resized a few parts and saved the file.

Image 4: a calculated cancel

It's fun to experiment with the KPT 3D Transform filter in the manner described above, because you never really know what to expect. But, there are other ways to bend filters...

After employing 3D Transform on a shape a couple of times, the result can be an extremely complex and processor-draining mass. Now, if Illustrator is safe from crashing, you can set up a filter once more and have it run.

Keeping an eye on the progress bar, go grab another cup of coffee and wait until the process is about halfway through. Then hit cancel. If you are not too early or too late (it's hard to tell sometimes) you can get some pretty cool results, where parts of the shape have been transformed and others have not.

Upon closer inspection of a successful run you can see patterns emerge, revealing how the filter runs from the outermost points of a shape first, moving towards the center – sort of like the rings of a tree stump. My suggestion would be to attempt this technique on a piece the perimeter of which is similar to a square, and which also has an insane surface to volume ratio with lots of nooks and crannies, much like the text I've been using above.

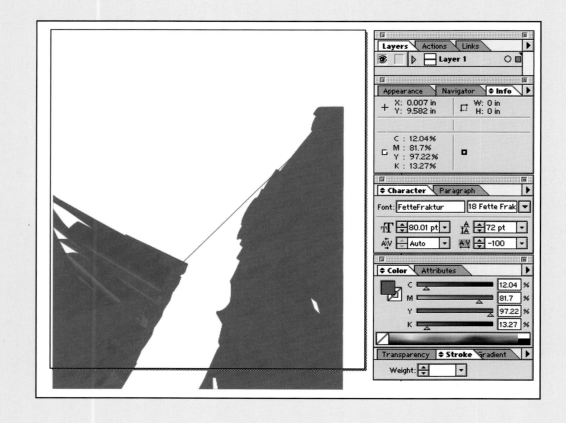

This is where having a somewhat slow machine can become an advantage. If you have the luxury of a huge super computer, you can try to fake it by opening all the memory-draining applications you can think of. The more your computer drags, the easier it is to step in and hit cancel at the right moment and achieve this effect. I liken it to a sort of controlled chaos, because you're never sure what the results will be (you can get a feel for them after a while, but they can't be pinpointed exactly), but you are able to recognize a pattern in the manner Illustrator filters convert a file. Of course, if your machine is *too* slow (maybe because you're rocking your dad's old Apple Lisa) the whole idea wears a bit thin, with an 'age' filter working its way across your face while you sit waiting for the ideal moment to hit cancel.

Image 5: wastin' time

Now, back to the task at hand. I continued repeating these experiments over and over again. Many of the results were a complete waste of time, but I knew eventually something valuable would be presented to me. I had been drinking a lot of coffee, so I was happy to carry on for a while.

As this is going to be a classic Prate/Gura design I punched in the word 'Prate', using some ugly, scripty font I have on my machine (I forget which, luckily). Next, I ran a 3D Transform on it with more of those tweaked out variables. After deleting a bunch of shapes and resizing it, I was left with a fairly unattractive result, which you can see below.

Instead of throwing up my hands and trashing the file, I pressed on, deciding that the best way to continue would be to remove more parts of the whole, then select the remaining elements and unite them (Effect > Pathfinder > Unite) into one solid piece.

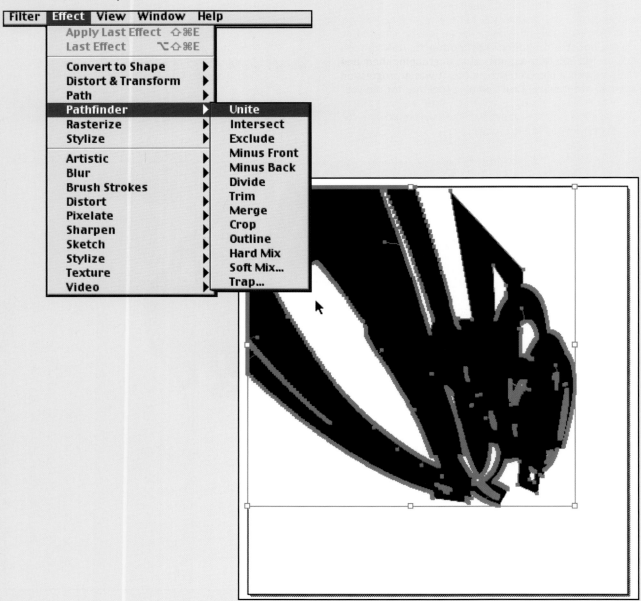

Uniting them into a solid shape helped reduce the file size; it also prevented me from ending up with too much of a mess, because I knew there was a long way to go before I would have a result that was acceptable.

I decided to change the color to one of the red/orange shades I'm fond of, and then ran another 3D Transform on it. I deleted 80% of the shapes after ungrouping them and was left with a completely new file. It was a progression of sorts, but it really wasn't coming together for me yet.

This provoked a flurry of activity. I ran another tweaked out 3D Transform, forcing a premature cancel, which gave me another big old mess. I ungrouped and removed yet more pieces of the resulting architectural shape, then converted the colors into a shade of brown.

Now, when I performed a 'blend' (filter > colors > blend horizontally), I learned something new: my 'force cancel' technique doesn't work on the blend filter. Still, sometimes you've got to have your hand pushed. Check out the progress report (right).

Moving on, I deleted more pieces of the file. I also selected parts and 'united' them, again for the sake of keeping the file size down because at this point there were too many irrelevant vectors in the mix. I took other parts and removed the color fill, leaving only outlines, as you can see in the screenshot.

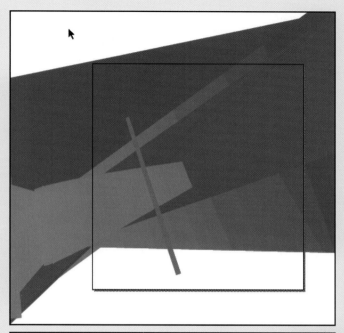

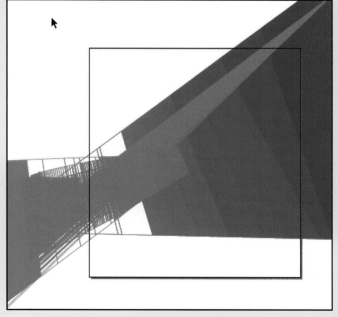

Now, I don't know what you're thinking but the brown color was starting to seriously get on my nerves, so I converted again, leaving me with a greenish-khaki toned piece, before 'uniting' more sections. When you use the 'unite' filter on sections with several colors, it chooses one of the more prevalent colors for the end result.

On the sections with outlines, I reduced the stroke thickness to 0.5, and resized a couple of the other sections, as below.

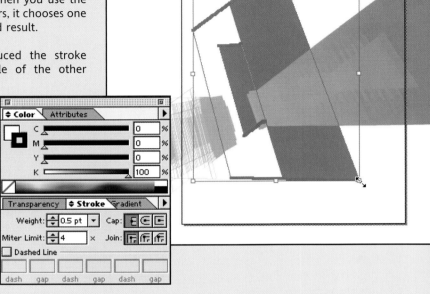

At this stage of development I realized that I wasn't impressed with the shapes, hated the color and was sick to the back teeth of looking at the image. I saved the file and moved on.

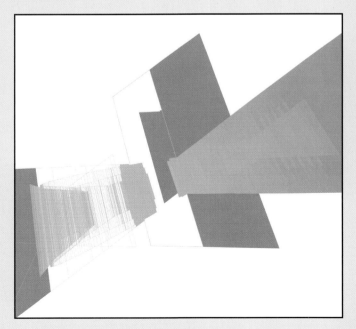

Image 6: rockin' the bevel

Employing the font called Text, in 74.2 point (a completely random number), I again typed the word 'Prate'.

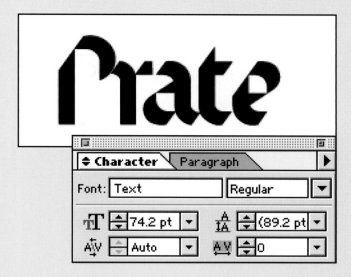

After converting the text to outlines, I brought it into the KPT 3D Transform plug-in, this time focusing on the bevel option. I set the bevel variable to the maximum possible and let the filter run. What resulted at first was quite an eyesore. The edges of each beveled letter overlapped the next, it had a terrible gray gradient and the word was completely illegible.

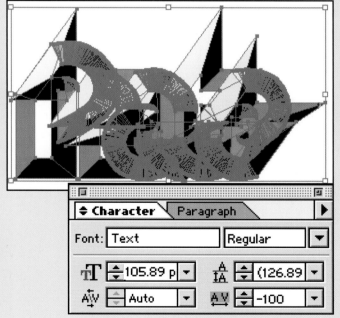

As I've already mentioned, when you perform a 3D Transform you are presented with front, back and joining parts of the image, forming a 3D effect. When you use a bevel, KPT creates a whole new piece, with the bevel becoming the fourth part, grouped by itself. This is the only piece of the result I was interested in, so I deleted everything else.

Now, I decided I could live with the overlapping and illegibility, but I couldn't handle the gray gradient. To counteract it I changed all the color fills to white, then added outlines.

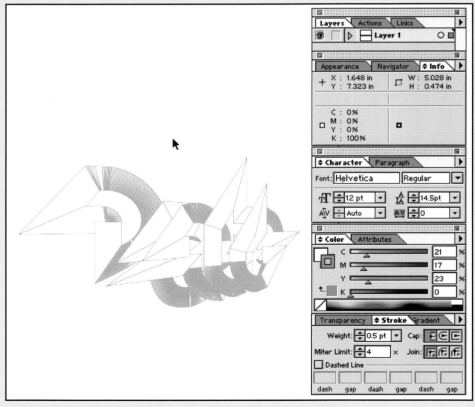

Still eager to experiment, I changed the stroke width on the outlines to 0.5 and skewed the shape slightly with a perspective coming from the right side of the canvas. I selected a muted light green-toned gray color for the outline.

This was finally the effect I had been looking for. I found it attractive and knew it complied with my sense of aesthetics, so I saved a copy of the file for later use and continued...

Image 7: generating my pattern

Still working with the open file, I decided to use it as a basis for a pattern. I spaced out the separate elements a bit (remnants of each character from the original word 'Prate') and united them.

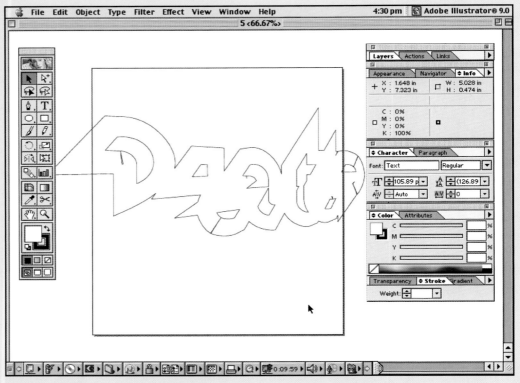

I then resized the result, much smaller than the previous incarnation, and rotated it 45 degrees.

I also took care to round both the 'cap' and 'join' on the outlines. I did this because I was planning to use the shape as a small and subtle pattern in the background of the final piece, and felt that sharp corners were useless on such a scale, taking away from the subtlety I would be trying to achieve later on. After this I once again saved and closed the file.

Take a break

Okay, I'm hungry now, so I call up Nina's on Meeker Avenue in Brooklyn. I order a small salad and a 'Nina's Italian Special Hero'. About 20 minutes later, the doorbell rings and my food is delivered. I remove 60% of the meat on the hero, eat till I am full and put the salad in the fridge for later on.

Image 8: learning from experiments

Using the font called Text, I typed out 'light&dark' and stacked it four-high. I then converted the text to outlines and colored it with a shade of red, before using a 3D Transform, using similar variables to the ones in the file for image 2.

In addition, I set the Highlight and Ambient options to shades of red, one being slightly darker and one slightly lighter than the red used on the original shape. After I ran the filter, I cleaned up the rogue shapes.

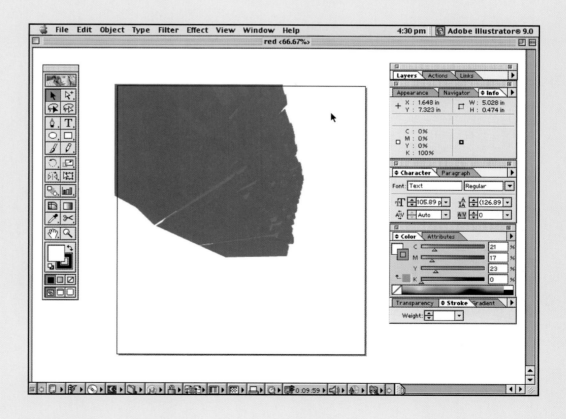

This was the sort of shape I was seeking as an addition to
my file library, so I saved it and closed the file.

Image 9: one final word

I thought I would attempt to make one more file, so I typed out 'light&and&dark' in the Fette Fraktur font I used earlier. I ran a 3D Transform on the type after I had converted to outlines. The original shape was black, so I set the Highlight and Ambient options to two very dark grays with slight blue tones to them. As described above I pushed the Perspective option way to the max... until KPT gave me its worried-looking warning message. After carefully removing several parts of the resulting shapes, I was left with two separate bodies made up of hundreds of little pieces.

The body of shapes on the left hand side was a little bland for my taste, and I felt there was little reason to bump up the file size with all these extra vectors, so I selected the whole shape and united it. Afterwards, I rotated the piece and placed the body on the right hand side of the canvas on top of it. I also stretched the shape a little.

That was about as far as this file was going to interest me, and I was getting anxious to start working on some compositions, so I saved and closed.

The composition

Image 3 was the file that I originally thought I would use as the basis for the final piece. The curves created using the black font were interesting... and I thought the shape and size would ensure an interesting 'positive versus negative space' ratio.

This decided, I opened the Image 3 file and started placing upon it the pieces from my library that I wanted to use. I masked the pattern so it would fit perfectly into the lower right corner and also started thinking about color.

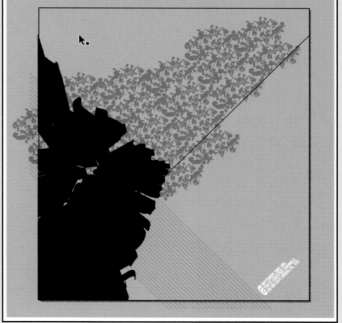

I placed a wallpaperish pattern on it that I made months ago (by scanning in a photo of a wall, taking it into Adobe Streamline, and cleaning it up in Illustrator). Then, I put the old pattern aside, and copy and pasted a single pixel line methodically (by holding down SHIFT and OPTION (or ALT) and tapping the up arrow a bunch of times).

After deciding the wallpaperish pattern wasn't working for me, I replaced it with the original pattern, moved the single pixel line stripes, fiddled with the color some more and finally decided it was time to stop working in Illustrator and open Photoshop.

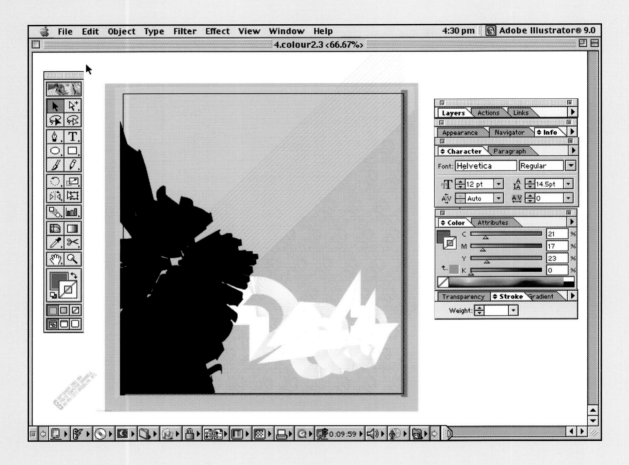

Firing up Photoshop

I opened Photoshop and created a new file, setting the size and resolution that I needed for the final piece, namely a 300dpi file at 8.25 x 9 inches.

I then proceeded to open and place files from my Illustrator library. I grabbed the file that went towards image 3, and started where I left off in Illustrator, adding and moving around elements from the library, fiddling with color and trying to keep in mind there shouldn't be too much obscuring of the remaining 'lightanddark' text that is still legible on the Fette Fraktur piece in image 3. After a while of doing this, I realized things weren't working out how I would have liked them to, so I replaced the image 3 file with the more mature red piece that makes up image 8. This was achieved by deleting the old layer, opening the image 8 illustrator file, then copy and pasting that into a new layer.

This is where things started to come together for me. I created a simple grid using the vertical guides. This spaced everything out nicely on the screen, and also encouraged me towards creating a gutter down the left hand side in the shape of a white bar, as you can see in the image below. I planned to use this space for supplementary information or text on the piece.

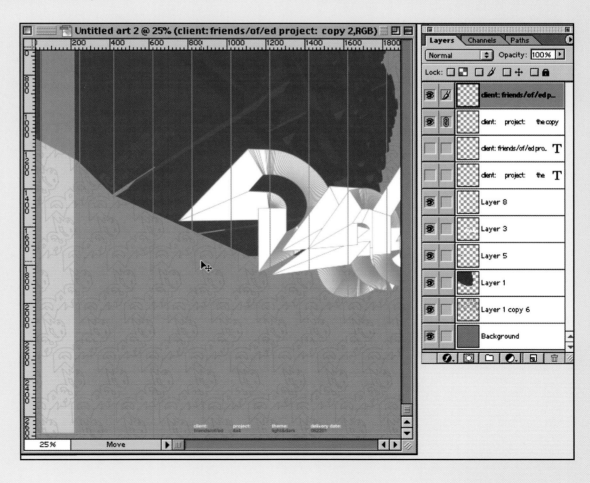

In order to create this supplementary text I used the font **Helvetica Neue** with the weight set to bold. The text I wrote described the purpose and delivery date for the piece. The top line was done in a red and the bottom line (in a separate layer) was written in white.

I rendered the type, by pressing CTRL while holding my mouse down on the "T" in the Layers Palette (which labels the layer as type) until a drop down box appeared, then selecting render layer. I then selected and spaced the copy making sure snap to grid was selected in the View drop down menu.

My next move was to rotate the two type layers 90 degrees counter-clockwise. I placed the text into the box I made earlier, lining it up with the grid and gutter. That's the guides done with for now, but they'll be useful again in a moment.

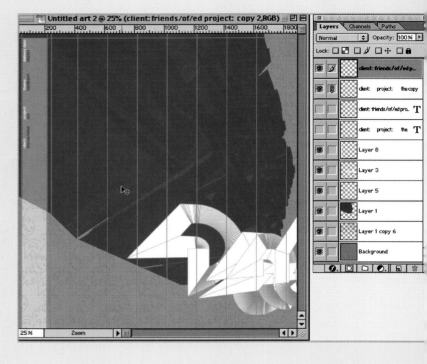

Following this I took the image 7 file and used it as the basis for a pattern in the background. This was done by careful copying, dragging and pasting of the initial pattern, holding down SHIFT to maintain straight lines.

There is a much easier, quicker and cleaner way to achieve this. Select the element you are using as the basis for the pattern then set it as the pattern by going up to the edit menu and selecting define pattern. The reason I chose the seemingly more difficult route was that my element wasn't equally spaced out, and instead of figuring out the math in my head to make the perfect selection to pattern the piece perfectly, I did it by hand.

Setting the layer to SCREEN (in the Layers Palette on the drop down menu for Layer Options) I dropped the transparency to 30%.

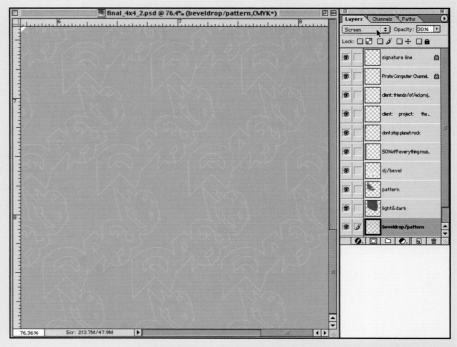

My thoughts turned now to the gutter box. I decided against using white as the color and chose a shade similar to the background. I then dropped the transparency to 50%, and moved the big red 3D text block down and over to the right slightly, using the trusty grid and gutter as guides.

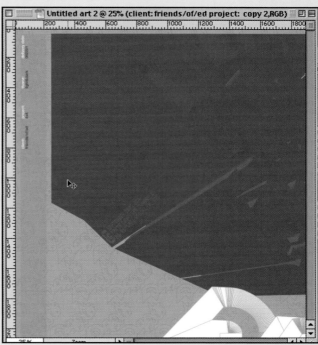

This wouldn't be a Prate/Gura design without a nice single pixel line covering the piece at a 45 degree angle. I used the color red and started from the bottom left going up to the top right hand corner. Then I chopped off the end so it would align with the red 3D text element.

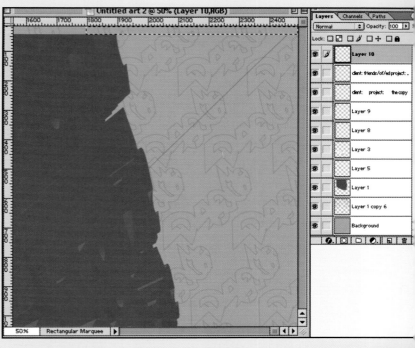

Turning my guides back on, I paid close attention to the bottom left of the piece, making sure the red single pixel line ended at the gutter and the white beveled element was snapped to the grid. I also added a line of copy, aligned to the guides.

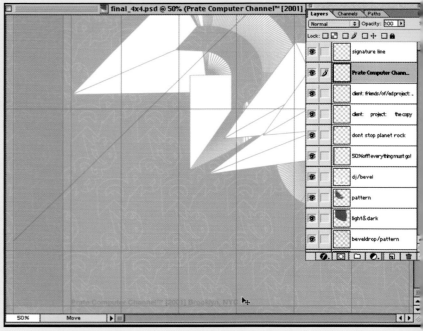

The final touch was to add a simple pixel pattern to the large flat planes facing the viewer on the red 3D text element. I used the Pencil tool to draw a very simple arrangement of pixels then, as mentioned earlier, I used the define pattern ability in the edit menu options list.

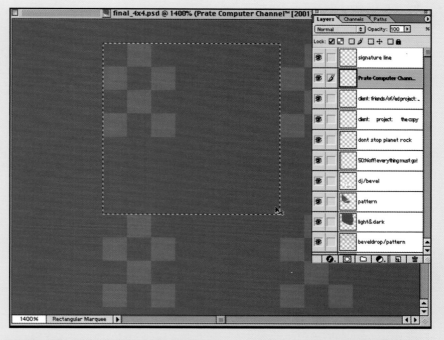

Using the Select tool I drew out a shape on the flat plane of the red 3D text element, went up to the edit menu options list, and selected fill. In the pop-up window I selected pattern in the drop down options and hit OK. After changing the hue (CMD U / CTRL U) slightly on one of the pattern areas, I was pretty satisfied.

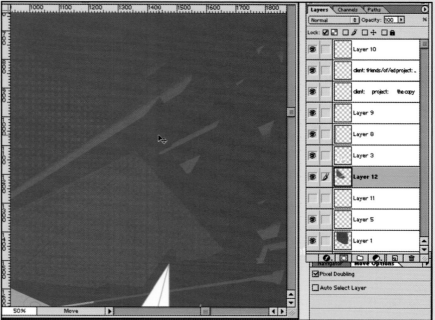

Final file

The point at which I am satisfied with the computer's results marks the finished piece for me. The technique that suits my working practices best is the creation of a library of images. I can plunder this library and rock whatever pieces of software I choose, to see how it responds and what kind of results it is capable of. As I've demonstrated, the drawback of a slow machine is not a drawback at all, and those ugly fonts can be used to make the most aesthetically pleasing forms.

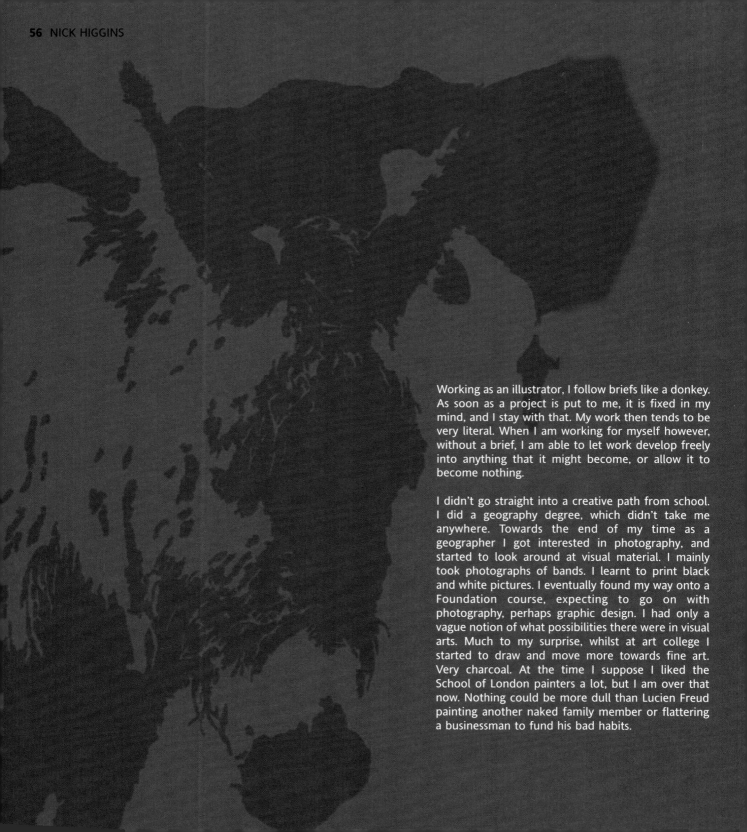

Working as an illustrator, I follow briefs like a donkey. As soon as a project is put to me, it is fixed in my mind, and I stay with that. My work then tends to be very literal. When I am working for myself however, without a brief, I am able to let work develop freely into anything that it might become, or allow it to become nothing.

I didn't go straight into a creative path from school. I did a geography degree, which didn't take me anywhere. Towards the end of my time as a geographer I got interested in photography, and started to look around at visual material. I mainly took photographs of bands. I learnt to print black and white pictures. I eventually found my way onto a Foundation course, expecting to go on with photography, perhaps graphic design. I had only a vague notion of what possibilities there were in visual arts. Much to my surprise, whilst at art college I started to draw and move more towards fine art. Very charcoal. At the time I suppose I liked the School of London painters a lot, but I am over that now. Nothing could be more dull than Lucien Freud painting another naked family member or flattering a businessman to fund his bad habits.

I was looking around at photographers all the time though. I remember the first time I saw William Eggleston's pictures, at the V&A. I thought they were shocking: I couldn't see the picture. What were they of? I came across them again later. I still think he is the most interesting photographer I have seen. I worked in a record shop for a long time. Occasionally a record went past with Eggleston's red ceiling picture (*Greenwood, Mississippi*) on it. Eventually I took it home and listened to it. It is a wonderful record, and a coincidence I still enjoy. I think that Eggleston has made me notice things, and take note of how things are arranged in front of me more than any other artist I have seen. I think he is intriguing and baffling. More recently the best photography book I have seen is Nicholas Faure's *Autoland*, a study of the motorway system in Switzerland. Again it makes you see how extraordinary the things that we pass all the time are.

Greenwood, Mississippi William Eggleston
© William Eggleston

I moved into illustration, because I wanted to do something that I could work at. Fine art, though it might have suited my portfolio at the time, was not going to work. The whole point of going back to college had been to get into some sort of visual art career. When I began working as an illustrator my medium of choice was usually collage. I spent hours cutting up copies of the National Geographic with nail scissors, finding images I could use. I did a lot of photocopying. Where I could, I also included my own photographs. My main focus was on landscapes, I worked by adding things until I got the scene that I needed. As I progressed with this style, I tried to use processes other than the photocopying, scissors and glue technique. I used transparent overlays, and photographic working methods. I

colored pieces by laying film over paint. I sketched on the back of acetate and then scratched through it. As I was developing these working methods, laser copiers meant I could start to manipulate the image within the photocopying process.

I was using old media to create these techniques of transparency and layering, and yet obviously they are exactly the techniques that can be employed instantly using a computer and Photoshop. But that realization came a long time before its actualization. It was a matter of computers and scanners becoming cheap enough, me finding some money, and a prolonged lull in commissions.

PIONEER

CONTAMINATED
WITH SEWAGE
KEEP OUT
AVOID ALL CONTACT
NO SWIMMING, WADING, SURFING OR WATER SKIING
COUNTY OF SAN DIEGO PUBLIC HEALTH SERVICES

In the meantime I started painting, and using other, very traditional, materials: wood, wire, clay, print and quite a lot of sewing. I started to paint a lot, in a loose, simple, brightly-colored way. I was very interested in certain specific points in history. The Mexican Revolution, the Crusades, and Lope Aguirre. They were stories that I thought were still contentious and still had a relevance today. I became very involved in the process and the research. I found a fantastic archive of pictures of the Mexican Revolution in the New York Public Library, where they allowed photocopying. Unfortunately, the work I did was commercially hopeless, and I could see no space for it in the fine art system. I still like a lot of the pictures though. Many of them are of particularly nasty scenes from those periods. At this point, the artist that I was most interested in was Sidney Nolan. I liked his use of historical incidents and the myths built up around them, and also his way of painting – as though he had to invent the whole process from scratch. His painting of Rimbaud at Harar is the last painting I saw that I was really overwhelmed by. I always used sign writers enamel paint, like he did, and got quite good at exploiting its strange effects when used incorrectly.

Rimbaud Sidney Nolan
© Sidney Nolan

Sewing was another traditional medium I worked in. I had seen picture of a collection of crosses in an encyclopaedia, and this suggested itself as a good subject for cross-stitch embroidery. From this I went on to machine embroidery. I really liked this medium because it had no conventions or familiarity; I could make up anything as I went along. I have not done any of this for a while, being too busy with commissioned work, and I miss it. I like art forms that are outside of what is usually seen in galleries. The most interesting exhibition I have seen in London for a long time was the Prinzhorn Collection of art from psychiatric hospitals in Germany. Everything in it was a self-contained invention, without any relation to conventions and schools.

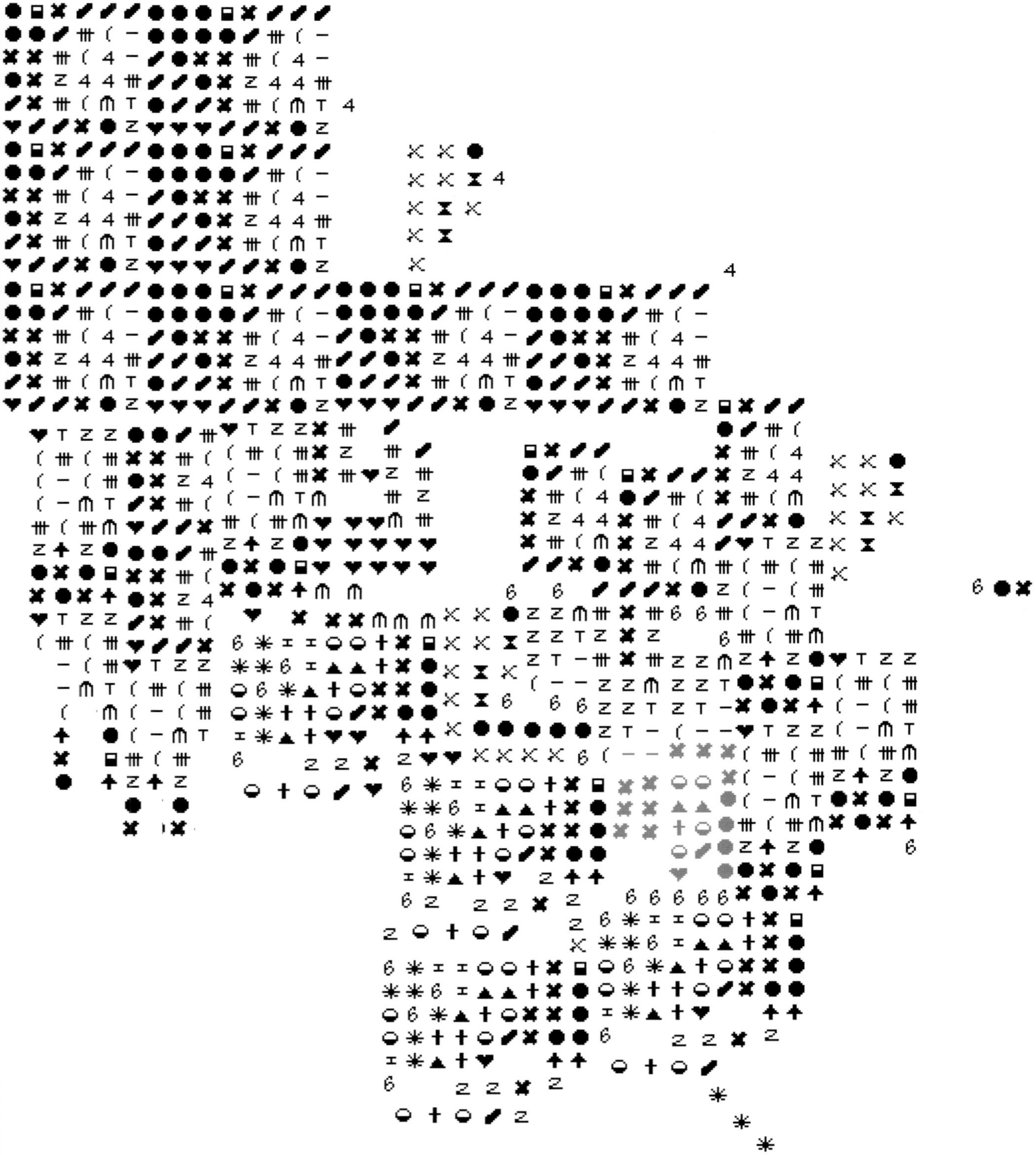

And now I work with a computer. This is partly an economic decision. It is what people are interested in, but as an illustrator it is also a way of being able to take over all the processes of manipulation that previously would have to have gone to a third party, like a printer or a photographic lab. I can manipulate images any way I like. My work on the computer does not have the narrative basis I pursued when painting. When I bought a Mac I had to learn to use it, and then develop a use for it. In a way I went back to what I had been doing before painting, using photography as the starting point for my work. But what was I going to do with the photographs? This new medium did not seem suited to the kind of work I had produced in paint.

Photographs are now my starting points, generating the inspiration and basis for my work. Without a brief to direct me, I think most of my interest lies in space and volume in pictures, whether real or illusory. I still find it almost impossible to complete a piece of work that doesn't feature a horizon. Compositions are drawn from real scenes but looked at as abstractions, emphasizing the parts that interest me. I try to arrive at a point where my picture makes an intriguing pattern. I want to emphasize my initial object of interest within the composition. It is largely a process of editing. Previously, with collage, I had created pictures by adding multiple elements together, sometimes using hundreds of components. Having pursued this direction for quite a while, I arrived at the profound conclusion that the fewer parts that make up the collage, the better.

I arrived at the same conclusion when I was painting, trying to stop working on a piece as soon as there was enough down on the canvas for the story to be apparent. Now, working with photographs in Photoshop, I have returned to collage mode, and the idea of fewer parts making a stronger whole is evident again. There is often an assumption that things made digitally will be complex, utilizing every last tool at the software's disposal. What I work on a lot of the time is stripping down a picture, removing all the elements that could be considered superfluous to the message of the piece. Along the way I may well add many parts from a variety of sources, but by the end I will have got rid of most of them. Recently, I have tried to use and edit just one photograph.

ARMY

Light & Dark is a theme that is so inclusive that it suggests nothing. I usually respond to shapes, volumes and patterns, physical, solid things. *Light & Dark* is less tangible, and a different kind of concept to work with. When I was given the theme I began my usual trawl through my hoard of photographs and images. It's quite an extensive collection now, covering my old paper-based ones, and a growing number of digital pictures, fairly randomly collected. I went through my photos, pulling out any that seemed to me to have some quality of light or dark as their focus of interest. Having chosen these, I put them into one file in order to start experimenting. Editing or combining them to make light or shadow the subject of the piece.

The work process I followed for these pieces was in fact similar to the way I worked on older collages using traditional methods. Layers and effects were applied, their order swapped around, elements were added and removed. Unsurprisingly though, more sophisticated changes are possible with Photoshop than can be performed with a photocopier, nail scissors and a four foot high pile of old National Geographics. Effects can be adjusted incrementally, where previously they were either present or absent. Binary, opacity, contrast, hue and saturation.... The list goes on. There are in fact more things to adjust than I would ever need to use. A lot of the filters, I think, are of no conceivable legitimate use, unless you are looking for a very ironic effect. (I'm sure you know the ones I'm talking about.)

Often I will start work with something in front of me: another artist's work, something that I think does the job I am attempting to do, or is at least going in the same direction. I have a lot of books, some of photography or painting. I like unselfconscious photography and illustration: technical books, natural history books, diagrams, old travel guides, plans and patterns. Books where the pictures are meant to illustrate, rather than work as independent compositions. I'm not sure how directly this impacts on my own work. Personally I don't do any graphic design work, but I am very fond of particular sorts of quite low-tech design. For example last Christmas in Casablanca I found a record shop fully stocked with Moroccan seven inch singles all in picture sleeves, which are lined up in front of me as I write. The frequent divergence from any original intention, as I allow the work to develop its own life rather than imposing a preconceived structure upon it, means that whatever I end up with probably bears no resemblance to the original influences.

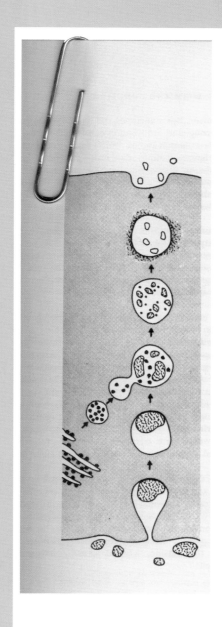

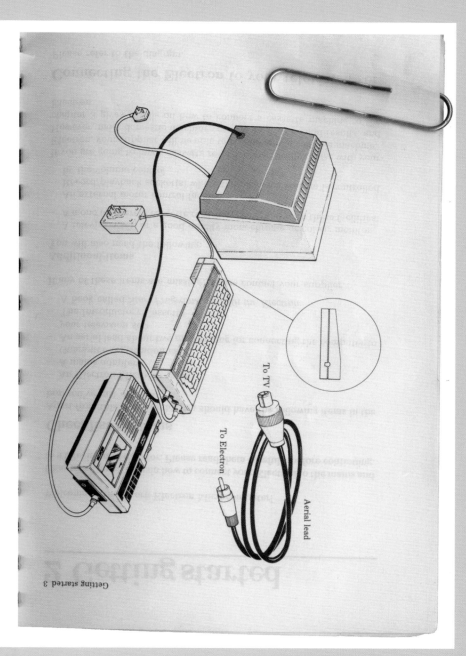

Whatever tools and materials I decide to work with, I rarely have any idea what I will end up with. Even when I have had a clear idea of what I thought I was aiming for, I am sure it has never worked out that way. I experiment with lots of different options, and at every stage there is the chance of something unplanned occurring. The editing process is often a case of getting rid of the bad accidents, but being open to including the good ones. I don't think I could maintain the interest if I knew from the beginning exactly where I was going. It was when I saw that computers were just as amenable to this less disciplined approach as traditional media that I decided I could use one to work on. I realize now that a computer is simply a tool, reflecting the judgment and taste of the user in exactly the same way a pencil or paintbrush does.

The Internet, I still see mainly as a way of sending work, rather than a forum to expose work in. I've nearly finished designing my own site, but it is really a portfolio on the web rather than a creative endeavor in its own right. I don't look at many web sites. Sometimes people forward addresses to me and I have a look. I think that I am more interested in content than techniques, and many web sites seem to have little relevance outside the world of web design. I am still a book person, but unfortunately as the supply of interesting second hand books seems to be drying up I may yet find that the web will start to take over.

I think I started to make work as a way of directly engaging with things that interest me. I wanted to know about the Mexican Revolution, so I painted it. I like certain patterns so I copy them. So the point of my personal work is often to extend my contact and continue a fascination with something. Copying things to be more familiar with them. I still like to draw in museums. I hope together with my artwork and tutorial, that this essay conveys some sense of how making imagery in any media, gives that very satisfying feeling of a direct involvement and control of a subject that interests you. And how the tools that we have can be used for invention by bending, re-arranging and organizing visual elements however you choose.

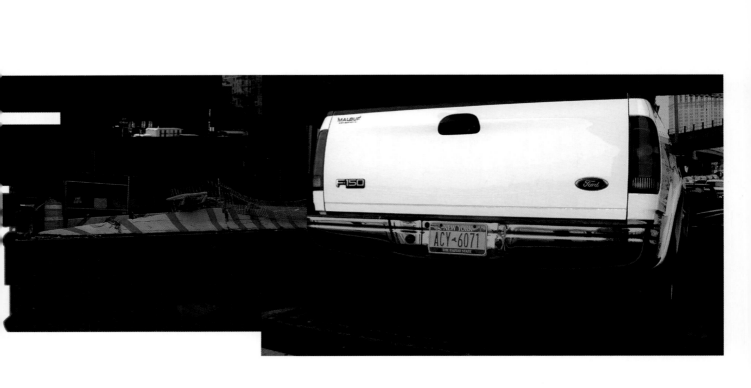

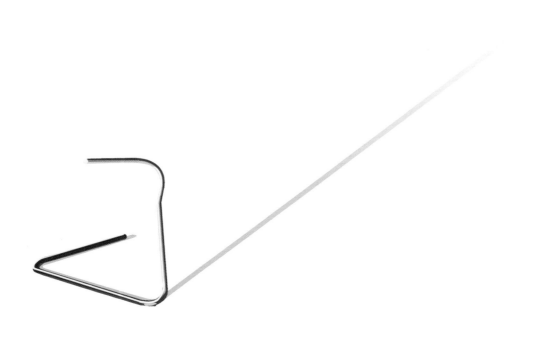

For this tutorial, I have ended up with three sections. I don't consider this a bad thing – indeed, it's fairly usual for me anyway: whether I am painting, collaging, or working in any other medium, I will make several starts – any one of which could be the one that goes on to be the finished piece. Others might be abandoned, or they might go on to assume their own identity, separate from whatever they started as.

I began my process by looking for some photographs that struck me as exemplifying some quality of light which made them relevant to the brief, and that I could work to enhance. The collection of files I ended up with was put into one folder, and this became my working library. This was the basis of my work, although I didn't shy from adding to it as the work progressed

Liberty

For this piece I wanted to make an abstract composition, starting with the idea of light and dark. All I knew was that I wanted something lambent. The first of my library pictures I decided to work with were *Floor* and *One*:

Floor had a very reflective character that I liked, and was just the sort of abstract image I wanted to use. *One* was a picture of One Liberty Plaza, which included a flower.

When I'm working like this, taking parts from some photographs and combining them with others, I have to be happy that I'm actually adding to each piece individually as well as creating a new picture with its own strengths. For example, when I actually started to put some of the pictures that I had initially considered suitable into combinations with the others, I found that they didn't work because their individual qualities were just too strong. They weren't enhanced by their juxtaposition with other parts, and they didn't add anything to the picture that I was trying to make. As with everything though, you don't know until you try.

Now that I had my initial images, it was time to make a start with my composition. First of all, I copied the parts of *Floor* and *One* that I wanted and placed them on separate layers in a new Photoshop file, 8.125 by 9 inches, 300 dpi.

I moved them into various relationships, trying each on top of the other, flipping them horizontally and vertically, and generally looking for an arrangement I was happy with:

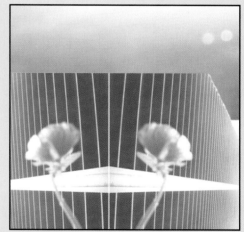

I found another file, *one2*, and pasted it into a new layer. This file was a photo of the same building from a little further back, which didn't include the flower. I flipped it so that it made a symmetrical perspective effect with *One*.

I worked with the two together for quite a while, before I got rid of *One*, and was left with just the plain building.

This is a perfect example of what I was talking about earlier. I like *One* as a picture in isolation, as I love the absurd relationship of scale between the big building and the little plant, but I could not make it work with other elements. They detracted from its strengths.

Already I was slipping into adding perspective to the piece, creating apparent pictorial depth, even though I had originally wanted to avoid this. I was aiming for a strong intriguing pattern that was abstract and evoked some quality of light.

A brief diversion

I decided that it still needed something more, so I looked for another image that could add to my picture. I found what I was looking for in a piece of sleeve art from a Beastie Boys record.

I selected the part of the image I wanted using the Rectangular Marquee tool, copied it and pasted it into my composition:

As a diversion, I also tried to reconfigure this fragment of a globe into a full sphere:

I had no intention of using this for my current brief, but it might come in useful somewhere else. I find it's worth following up creative ideas whenever they occur. A lot of the time, these offshoots will provide you with new and intriguing ammunition for your future projects.

I shuffled and adjusted my three pictures for a long time, trying to make one and one and one add up to something greater than three. Unfortunately, they were reluctant to cooperate.

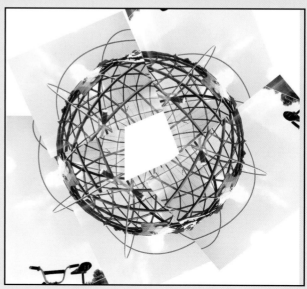

Twisting paper clips

As I have said, I'd just allowed myself to put some perspective into the picture. With this in mind I began to work on another element. Just taking a paper clip and unfolding it always fascinates me, as I find the resulting change from flat to volumetric somehow magical. I used a photograph of just such a spoiled paper clip and traced over it in Illustrator, adjusting the paths to fit the clip.

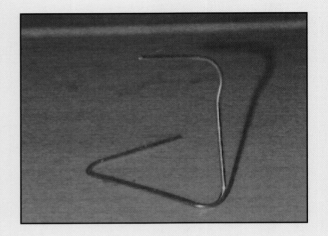

I then took this drawing into Photoshop and pasted it as a path into a new file.

I use paths a lot, sometimes in Illustrator, then importing them into Photoshop, and sometimes just using the path tools in Photoshop. I like paths because they allow me to make accurate drawings – and even more because they allow me to draw quite badly, and then use the handles and beziers to drag the drawing into the shape that I want it. It is a very time-consuming process, but very forgiving. It teaches patience!

As I imagine you'll have found out by now it's very hard to create an accurate image drawing with the mouse. I find that even with a pen and graphics tablet, I don't get a very satisfactory rendering from the pencil or brush tool. I like the perfect curves and line weights that you can get by using a path and stroking it. They are one of the strengths of the computer as a tool.

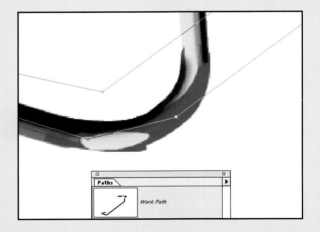

Generally speaking, the other, and perhaps most useful, reason for using paths in Photoshop is their indifference to resolution; that is, as vectors, I can scale them up or down, and maintain the quality of the line.

Anyway, back to business. I wanted to use Photoshop for the next part of the process, because I find it easier to use its coloring tools and effects than those of Illustrator. In fact, I use Illustrator less and less these days ever since the path tools in Photoshop were improved.

Using the path I had imported, I colored the drawing by filling it with some gray shading, using the paint bucket tool, and then added some highlights. I created them by using the Line tool, (create filled region option, weight 1 pixel, anti-alias checked,) and then using a Gaussian blur to soften the edges (Filter > Blur > Gaussian blur, radius 1 pixel).

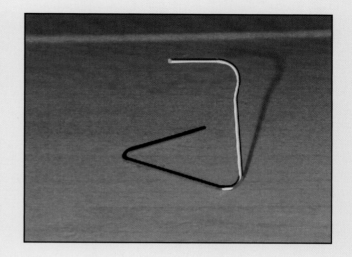

Now that I had my drawing of a clip, I needed to see how I could use it to add to the quality of my composition. First of all, I selected it using the Magnetic Lasso tool, (it helps to zoom in for doing this kind of job) and copied it into a new layer, and I was immediately more interested in this element than the others. With this addition though, the composition was starting to feel cramped – something had to go. After some careful consideration, I decided that the globe was the weakest component, and so I removed it. I was now back to only three pieces, but something still wasn't right. I tried to leave the clip against the receding form of *one2*, but to no avail:

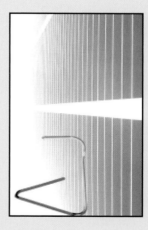

I realized that the addition of the artificial, drawn element of the paper clip had completely changed the nature of the entire image. The more natural photographic parts now no longer seemed suitable. With this in mind, *one2* was the next piece to go. I replaced it with some sky, and a white, artificial block:

I created this by making a selection of the size and shape that I wanted, and then pasting some sky into it. Using the Rectangular Selection tool, I defined the area that would become the sky, and then cut out the shape of the white block using ALT and the Selection tool. I found another picture, called *Lamp*, that I thought had a suitable sky with a nice tonal quality:

I copied this sky from *Lamp* and used the Paste Into command to make it fill the selection that I had prepared. I also decided to try and add some volume to the block by drawing a gray side on it to make it feel solid, using the Line and Paint Bucket tools. I decided though to leave its perspective in question to let the viewer make a decision:

To fill up the space that was now prominent at the front of the composition, I copied and pasted *Floor*, flipping it horizontally to fill up the full width of the space:

The last element that I added was a shadow cast by the clip. I created a new layer, and then used the Polygonal Lasso tool to draw a suitable shape:

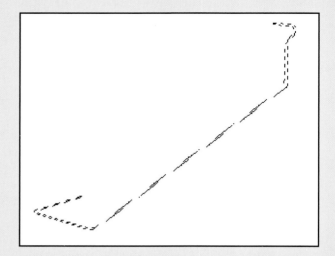

I then filled this shape using a Foreground to Transparent gradient. This allowed the shadow to fade out atmospherically, and it also handily solved the problem of working out exactly how the curved clip's shadow should fall. Since the shadow was on its own layer, I was able to adjust its opacity separately. I decided to set the layer's opacity to 25%.

Having done all of this, I was happy with the picture, and believed it to be complete. I had a simple, slightly strange picture that I hoped had a slightly surreal atmosphere, mildly ambiguous scale, and of course enough light and dark qualities to satisfy the brief.

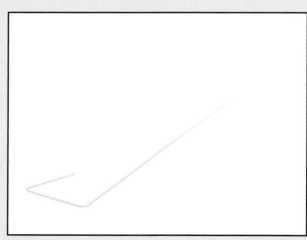

It turned out that it wasn't quite as complete as I'd believed. When I returned to the composition to compile my notes on the process, I decided that it still wasn't quite doing what I wanted. I turned off one of the layers containing half of *Floor*, and was much happier with the composition. It was now far more interesting, as I felt that its flat pattern set against the ambiguity of its spatial illusion was somehow stronger than before:

Having worked with many elements, I was pleased with the extreme simplicity that I had arrived at. I think that computers often seduce people into over complicating pictures, and it's sometimes worth trying to make things out of as few pieces as possible – it's funny how you can add so much to an image by just removing a part of it.

Wash

The second picture I created in this series is called *Wash*, which started out as a picture of a car wash in New York. This car wash was in a strangely prominent position on a corner of Broadway, and it was covered with rows of flashing lights blinking 24 hours a day, deliberately bathing itself in a huge pool of light:

It's not the sort of picture that I normally work with, as it's just way too picturesque. The subject, becomes too interesting, too exotic, and overwhelms the subtler things that interest me, in particular the simple shape and actual construction of the object. I decided to work with it though, because if *Light & Dark* was to be the theme of the work, then it was a most deserving candidate.

I decided that what I wanted to do with it was to emphasize the glow and the brightness in the image radiating out from what is in fact rather a banal subject. To begin with I needed to isolate the bright parts of the image, so I selected the central piece of the photo (the part I wanted to keep) and then selected the inverse (cmd + shift + I / ctrl + shift + I) and filled it with black.

I wanted to make the bright section even brighter. To do this, I increased the contrast of the image, beyond a comfortable level so that almost all that remained was pure light and dark, with hardly any shading.

Using the Magic Wand tool, I selected some of the dark part of the image, chose Select Similar, and then Select Inverse to give me all of the light parts.

I copied this new selection, and then used the History palette to go back to the image as it was before I changed the contrast. I then pasted my bright selection into a new layer.

To try to enhance the glow of the lights, I copied this light layer again, and put a Gaussian Blur on it. I now found, though, that I was beginning to bleach out the yellow taxi, and so I needed to give it some more definition. In order to do this I drew around it with the Magnetic lasso tool and made a new layer, then filled the selected taxi shape with yellow and reduced its opacity to blend it in with the existing image:

I tried to arrive at a completed image with these four layers, but even when I was reasonably happy with the picture itself, it still just had a little too much of that picturesque quality that I wasn't happy with. I wanted to change its atmosphere entirely, so I increased the canvas size to give me a bit of space to work with, and then looked at some other pictures that I had scanned which might combine well with the car wash.

Pitching in extra images

I found a picture of the back of a pickup truck, which was taken from quite a low viewpoint behind the vehicle:

The upshot of this is that it's really just a picture of one panel, and this was the reason I liked it. It had reduced the car to a quite abstract view of just one of its parts. Single car panels have a distinctly odd look about them, which is something I've picked up from Richard Prince's work with car hoods.

I have quite an ambivalent relationship with cars, in that I like them because few things are as effective in evoking a particular time and place, which is very useful as an illustrator, but on the other hand, I like bicycles and despise car culture. I do admit though, they have their uses...

As well as the car, I wanted to choose something that would add a background to the picture. Yes, I was going for a horizon! I had a nice picture of some skyscrapers in New York at dusk, which would really emphasize the light and dark aspects of the image.

The different elements were initially put together quite arbitrarily in scale and position, just so I could get a rough idea of what they looked like together. I then moved them around until I'd achieved a pleasing composition. I felt that the car panel was becoming the strongest element in the picture now, so I scaled it to reflect its importance.

After spending a lot of time working on the original car wash picture, it was now only one of three elements in a larger composition, and the one I was least happy with. I moved it around and altered its size trying to find somewhere it would fit, but before long I realized that I would never like it, as its picturesque nature would never work. Without further ado, I got rid of it, and settled on a relationship between the car and the landscape behind. I had spent a lot of time on the car wash, but if it wasn't going to work, then it had to go. As was the case in the last composition, I find that it's better to use the smallest number of pieces that can do the job rather than cluttering and over-complicating things.

Having said that, when I removed the car wash, I began to feel that the picture needed something more. I had the main subject of the composition in the form of the car panel, and I had my background. Now what I really needed was a third element, a middle ground to connect them. This picture was fast becoming a fabricated urban landscape, so I wanted to thematically link the car with the city.

What do cars and cities have in common? Roads. I have a big interest in road works and road furniture at the moment. I love the fluorescent hazard tape and traffic cones, and piles of paving slabs stacked up in the street, so luckily I have a lot of photographs of road works. I like to see pleasing compositions of hazard furniture and holes in the road, and the feelings they evoke. I want to know if people working on the roads stand up and look at the long lines of traffic and think, with the pride of a master craftsman, "I made that!"

Whatever, all that really mattered was that I had just the photograph to make up the middle ground for this picture.

After that, it was just a matter of arranging the layers to find something that I was happy with, and in this case, it didn't take too long.

One thing that I noticed when I'd finished the work was that the entire composition was made from pictures taken in America. This is no bad thing, but, viewed through English eyes, it can lend the picture a slightly exotic air. As I have said throughout, I very much wanted to avoid being picturesque so I was worried that the location gave the image too much charm. In the end though, I decided it was okay, the picture represents space, objects observed in a very direct way, and the way that light and dark affect this arrangement.

When I look back on it, the picture reminds me slightly of William Eggleston's work.

I really like his photographs, but, particularly from a British point of view, I always see the exotic location of the southern states of America as a dangerous intrusion. It's too easy for me to be diverted by an archaic truck or an elegantly wasted road sign, and lose sight of the picture as a whole.

It's difficult to pin down what Eggleston's subject is, but it never seems like it should be cultural charm, or nostalgic recognition. This is borne out by the fact that when his pictures include views of very familiar parts of London, any such distraction, for me, is gone. It's worth just being aware that no matter how small the world can sometimes feel in the Internet age, it's still a hugely contrasting place, and no matter how inconsequentially common something may seem to one person, it will always be alien to another.

Light

The last piece in my disparate triptych is called *Light* and it begins with a picture of a footbridge across a railway:

It was taken in the evening, and I particularly like the quality of light. The sky is still bright, but the bridge and platform are in shadow and the lamps are lit. I think it's very atmospheric.

Straightening out nature

Having identified this as an interesting photograph for its qualities of light and dark, I wanted to use Photoshop to emphasize what I saw, to exaggerate it, to cheat. I wanted to push up the contrasts and provide a sort of hyper-real filter to the original. My instinct was to work on the area between the sky and the bridge, making them perfectly separate from one another.

The first thing I did was to redraw the edges of the bridge and sky, making perfect borders between them. For this batch of actions I employed the Rubber Stamp tool and the Line tool, together with the Polygonal and Regular Selection tools. First off, I'll go with the Rubber Stamp.

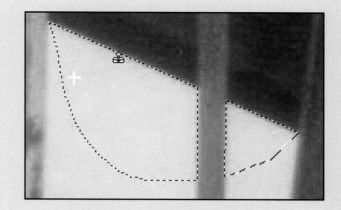

Having made my selection along the border between the light and dark, I used the Rubber Stamp tool to paint right up to the edge, eliminating the photograph's blur between edges. To further emphasize this effect, I inverted my selection (shift + cmd + I / shift + ctrl + I) and painted the other side of the edge too.

What I'm doing here is making perfect borders, ones which couldn't and wouldn't be there in a photograph, and which you wouldn't see in real life if you were there. I realized as I was doing it that what I was making was a surreal version of what I want to be there, something more perfect than is possible.

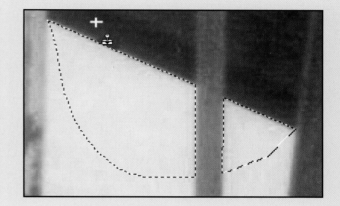

After carrying out this bit of perfectionism, I straightened things up using the Line tool. This tool can be a bit intrusive, so I employed a softening technique. Using another edge between light and dark (in this case the top of the shelter at the foot of the steps) I took an Eyedropper full of the darker color, then set the Line tool opacity to about 85%. This stopped it appearing hard and separate from the rest of the picture. Then I held down the shift key as I drew the line to enforce perfect verticals and horizontals wherever possible.

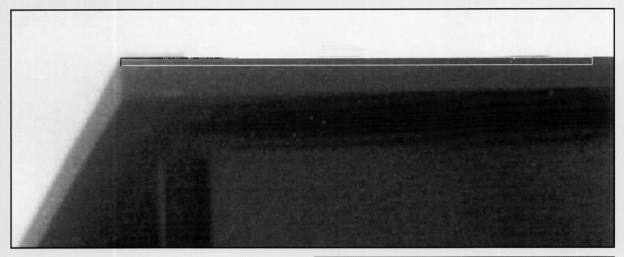

The big picture

Having ruled the picture in this way for a while, I started to look at the composition as a whole, keeping an eye out for particular areas that I liked or disliked. You can see the kinds of things I changed by comparing the original picture with the final picture. For example, I didn't think the white pole was useful, so I got rid of it. To achieve this, I used the Straight Line Lasso tool to draw exactly around the borders that would contain the area of sky that I would draw in to cover up the pole. Then I used the Rubber Stamp tool to paint sky over the pole, being careful not to leave any strange unnatural repeated marks in the sky.

Another thing I didn't like was the way that the steps up the bridge were indistinct and not horizontal, so I redrew them. I did this simply using the Line tool set to 65% opacity. What can I say? I don't know why I chose this figure. I just prefer certain percentages to others for no good reason. I use 65% a lot, but never 55%. Whatever your own chosen percentage, I suppose the reasoning for it is to have some texture left within the line, and not just a solid color. The difficulty with this process is to be persistent and meticulous enough for the amendments to be noticeable. I want them to be subtle, but definitely noticeable. In this instance the surreal or hyper-real effect constitutes a tricky balancing act.

Having redrawn the steps, I then needed to also perfect the handrails. I wanted to make their edges sharper, and their color more uniform. I started by making a selection of the main parts of the rails with the Rectangular Marquee, and then adding on the ends freehand using the regular Lasso.

Having done this for each rail, I then made a new layer, and filled the selections with my chosen foreground color. Adding this color into a new layer means that I can alter its opacity as much as I like without altering the character of the rail below it. This is all made possible by one of Photoshop's neat little touches, the ability to change layers without losing the current selection. By this means, the final appearance of the rails was achieved by switching between the translucent colored layer above and the actual picture of the rails below, adjusting them both until I was happy with the results.

A tip that I have found useful on many occasions is to save a selection like this (through select > save selection), particularly if it's been complicated to draw, in case you want to re-adjust this same area later. Each selection saved will be collected up in the document and ready for use any time you open it up. The small amount of space this takes up on your hard disk is easily justified by the amount of time and frustration you save by not having to painstakingly redraw the selection. To recall it, just choose select > load selection and it will pop back up on your screen.

After satisfying myself with the color and clarity of the lines, I then set to work on their alignment. I noticed that the rails ended unevenly, so I used a rectangular selection to line up their ends.

After doing this, I used the Rubber Stamp to move the right-hand end up a bit to align it perfectly with the left. Why did I do this? I suppose I was trying to impose a sort of uniformity onto the picture, to make it as rigid as a diagram. However, you should watch out when performing this kind of a task. It's easy to destroy the perspective on an image and leave it looking wrong. No problems here, though.

I also perfected the edges, and flattened the tone, of the backs of the signs in the picture. As with the steps and the rails, this was just a process of selecting the sign, rubber-stamping the edges to straighten them and using the Line tool as previously described to ensure they were perfectly horizontal or vertical if required, and then flattening the tone by filling the selection with a foreground color at 65% opacity. I also found that I didn't like one of the signs, so I got rid of it by creating a selection around it, and then filling it with some texture taken from the side of the bridge.

This process of perfecting lines and flattening tones went on throughout the picture wherever I thought it was necessary, this was especially important in some areas of the picture where the tones were very similar. In these cases I wanted to make the surfaces more obvious. For example, the faces of some of the concrete fence posts, and the sides of the bridge all had to be defined. I also adjusted the brightness and contrast of some surfaces to define them and separate them from their neighbors.

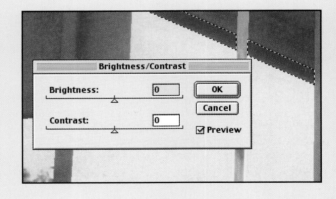

Sky

Once I'd corrected the man-made elements, I turned to my next major task – improving nature. Something needed to be done with the sky to emphasize the contrast between it and the ground. I used the Magic Wand to select all of the sky. (Magic Wand is such an unsatisfactory name for this tool. I teach basic Photoshop, and always feel that I have to explain that it is not actually magic. People are always so disappointed). Given that there is a strong contrast between the light of the sky and the rest of the picture, it was easy to select all of the sky with several clicks of the wand.

The only problem area was around the trees, and here it was necessary to draw in some loose, vegetal edges with the Lasso tool.

Having done this, I made a new layer, and filled this selection with blue. It didn't actually have to be blue because I was only going to use it as a mask to select either the sky, or invert it to work on all other areas. When I'd finished, my mask looked like this:

The result of this is, as you'll notice, much the same as if I had saved the selection I made of the sky through select > save selection. However, sometimes I like to have a solid mask to help me define different areas that I expect to work on repeatedly. Having defined the sky, I copied and pasted it as a new layer. I then adjusted this layer for brightness, contrast, and color. I could also have adjusted its opacity, but in this case I felt it was better left at 100%.

I've already mentioned the initial problems I had with the trees when selecting the sky. Trees are always very difficult things to work with in Photoshop, and I thought about getting rid of them completely. Given a rainy day and not much to do I would try it – as they are, like hair, very difficult to put a satisfactorily naturalistic edge around.

Starting with the inverse of the sky selection, I removed everything but the trees, and pasted this selection into a new layer. I then filled this selection with green and adjusted its opacity. I wanted to avoid a sharp, unnatural block of green, so I used the Eraser to roughen the edges, giving the illusion of individual leaves, and deleting any rogue areas of green in the sky.

I have to admit that this is the least satisfactory part of the process, and I'm still not convinced that the bushes are blandly natural enough for the tone of the piece.

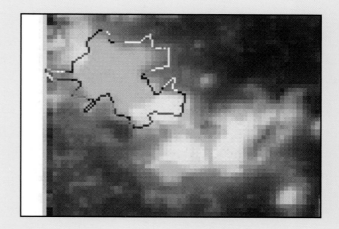

Ground

I wanted to emphasize the flat ground areas in the picture, and to even out the tones in them. These were easy to select with the Polygonal Lasso tool. They were then pasted into another new layer, and filled with a concrete color. I actually used a graded fill for the ground to give it a sense of perspective, fading as it goes into the picture. I then adjusted the layer's opacity to keep the textures present in the picture right:

Finally, I did the same perfect line and flat tone routine to some other parts of the image, such as some of the poles and posts. Here's a look at the final adjustments, including the sky mask that I made, without the background behind them so you can see them clearly:

I considered this pretty much finished except for the endless fiddling around and sharpening edges, which always goes on until the work has to be delivered. It is, as I said, a question of persistence to make the thing more and more uniform, more and more noticeable.

With the benefit of a little break, I returned to the work with fresh eyes. I realized that it no longer had the contrast between light and dark, and sky and non-sky, that had been the original intention of the picture.

I made a copy of the file, and used the Merge Visible command (shift + cmd + E / shift + ctrl + E) to flatten every layer except for the sky mask layer, which I had hidden.

I then turned the sky mask layer back on and selected it. A quick use of the Select Inverse command left me with a marquee around the ground. I then hid the sky mask layer again, and used the Brightness and Contrast controls to darken the ground again. I felt that the resulting image looked satisfactory, and fulfilled my original aims.

In conclusion

Photoshop for me, in the sort of work I have done here, works just like painting or collage, in that I can reproduce the world just as I want it. I can emphasize what I am interested in, and delete entirely anything I think is a distraction. From this I can create an image or elements from various images, making an attractive picture to design around or illustrate with.

It can, I realized as I was doing these pieces of work, also produce a certain sort of surrealism. Not the "tigers-swimming-around-a-lollipop-just-before-my-mother-woke-me-up" kind, which I don't find very interesting, but the juxtaposition of the unexpected with the familiar. The wrong sky, the wrong scale, the wrong thing in the wrong place. Photoshop as a re-touching and compositing tool obviously works very well in this way.

As a drawing tool, I am not so sure. I have not yet found a completely satisfying way of generating drawings within the programs. This is due partly to a preference for hands-on methods: I like biros and pencils and paintbrushes, and the feeling of using them. Also, I think that I have not yet overcome the abstract notion of scale that is enforced working on the computer. I like, at the moment, to make big drawings, full of little things. I know I could do these perfectly easily on the computer, and then get them printed out, but at the moment I still need to see them as I am making them.

I also feel that I have not yet found a way of using the computer to make art with the personality of some of my previous work. Perhaps I am just old fashioned in my judgments and tastes, but I cannot find a way of making work with the charm of paintings, embroidery, drawings in ink, or painting on glass. I think the fact that the final work exists only as a printout, or on screen, limits what I feel I can achieve. This would obviously not be a problem for someone with a background in film, video or graphics, but I am nostalgic for materials, I suppose. When allowed the luxury of describing my work and its development process that this book provided, I kept wanting to show some sewing, just for balance.

Having said this, I wouldn't want to give a false impression of my feelings about Photoshop and computer art generally. Working digitally has so many advantages, and makes so many processes instantly accessible, that it has changed what I do completely. I have also become far more commercially viable as an artist.

Instead of making my way to the coffee shop via the Pacific Coast Highway I prefer to take the side streets. The alleys are calm, empty except for a few people walking their dogs or enjoying a stroll. The pace of life seems relaxed, the people united by a common goal; to enjoy the day and whatever it brings. The journey is as important as the destination.

The coffeehouse is a cool place because it doesn't look like a café. If you were to pass it on your way to work you might think it was a little bookstore. The only people that know of the coffeehouse are the locals, and the odd person who's wandered in off the street. It's in a place like this that I can really find my thoughts. I try to find a table off to the side. If there is a band playing, all to the good. I get lost in the music and my own thoughts. There is no-one to answer to and nothing to distract me. I'm free to explore my own ideas and let concepts ripen in my mind.

pacific coast highway

boardwalk @ laguna beach

As a student I concentrated on the medium of print with minimal emphasis on new media and web design. But new media made a huge impact on me when I first experienced it. During my final years as a student at the Art Institute of Southern California I became aware of the massive scope of the Internet and multimedia for freedom of thought and personal expression. It was a whole new intellectual space for people to express their creativity.

I started using Photoshop 3.0 in 1996. Since then I have developed knowledge of the application that has allowed me to be comfortable in the pursuit of problem solving. The introduction of computer-based design packages has just thrown open the field as far as artistic expression is concerned. It provides so many tools to realize the intricacies of the mind's visions.

Five years ago in order to create a Photoshop image using my own photography, the preparation would have taken three or four days, with manual photo shoots, film development, professional drum scanning, and a top of the line Macintosh loaded with RAM able to cope with this kind of work. And that's just to start a new Photoshop document using your personal source imagery. Today if I come across some inspirational subject matter all I have to do is pull out my handy little Canon S-10 digital camera, take about 20 high resolution shots of the subject, bring it back to my machine, snap in the USB cable to the camera and boom, the images are on my desktop. It's amazing. I am now able to produce three or four days' worth of work in approximately 15 minutes thanks to the latest developments in technology. This is my inspiration to get out there and shoot some imagery for my work. I do not see myself as limited to Photoshop, but I certainly feel at home with it, and it creates a multitude of possibilities.

Coffee shop @ laguna beach

laguna beach

lunch - 1pm

When I was a child, I felt so free. And it wasn't until recently that I asked myself where that feeling had gone. I have been working as a professional contracting designer since 1997. Straight after college I became very involved in the corporate design world. I went in deep, and began to lose what I had worked so hard to achieve. I had worked on everything from simple business cards to a three day creative proposal worth 4.2 million dollars for the third largest insurance company in the country. I had gone from junior designer to senior designer to art director.

I remember gazing out of the office window one day, watching the people driving along Wilshire Blvd. in a daze, wondering whether they knew what they looked like from my perspective. And at that point, I got up and walked to the bathroom. The water was cold on my face. As I dried my hands and looked in the mirror I saw a glimpse of who I used to be. The boy that used to ditch school and head to the beach. "But look at me now," I thought. I had lost the feeling of freedom and beauty that had drawn me towards art in the first place.

This was the turning point for me. It was time for me to make a change. Thankfully, I was able to make the transition back to freelance. It was like putting on my most comfortable pair of sweats. Every morning is a new morning. Working freelance I am given the chance to experience life and all that it has to offer. There is no commute to the studio. There are no appointments at 7:15 in the morning 62 miles from the house. And there are no ridiculous and uncomfortable client meetings. All I have to do is find a few reliable clients, do a little work for them, and the rest of the time is mine. I spend it with my family, (my wife Amber and son Derek are an inspiration to me), hit the waves for a surf, or head to the foothills for a good six mile mountain bike ride. At this moment, we are living in Dana Point California. I am exactly one mile from Salt Creek Beach, which offers some really good waves. And believe me, I'm saying all of this with a smile. It's a joy living my life like this.

As a teenager, I loved trekking down to the beachfront in the Fall. I remember I used to ditch school and run down to the bus stop in the morning with bodyboard in hand. At the beach the seagulls would hang around in the sky and swoop to just feet from where you stood. As I looked at my watch I thought of what class I was supposed to be in at the time. Then a smile would come to my face. I would be in the water for hours. Even if a perfect wave rolled by and I couldn't catch it, there wasn't a worry in the world. Because even though I had my wetsuit and fins on and I was bobbing around in the cold ocean water, that wasn't why I was there. I was there to experience the freedom of the day. Every single day offers an amazing wealth of freedom.

The best work happens when you are relieved of all your worldly pressures, and you are at liberty to create. Do you remember the amount of anxiety and stress that was released from your shoulders every time the final school bell of the day rang in elementary school? Remember how relaxed you were as you rode your bike home in the evening? It was as if the rest of the day was going to be a breeze from that point on. In this respect, try to define where the space for that may be in your life. And if you have trouble finding it, take a good look at where you are and try your best to create it.

I feel my true body of work comes from experimental solutions. I get excited when people come to me asking me to reveal my experimental work, rather than my portfolio. If they come to me asking for that, they just might be interested in seeing more. Imagine working all day and night on experimental artwork! Imagine the possibilities, if this could be the main priority in life. There are times when I can sit down and just work for hours. I have a hunger for producing something new and different from anything I have seen before. I am not satisfied with creating work that simply functions. There is no achievement in that. My interest lies in creating vehicles for inspiration.

Light and dark, Light and dark, Light and dark... it's been ticking away in my mind all weekend. Before I began this project, I didn't think I had a process behind my concepts. For some reason I was eager to claim that I was involved in a freestyle type of movement with my concept development. But the more I think about it, I realize I do have a process.

When I am handed a new project, it's exciting. I feel as though I have been graced with another chance to do my best, to push my abilities to the limit. But I always get nervous and jittery, so when I get given the theme, I immediately set it aside. Rather than brainstorming right away, I try my best to relax and let ideas develop organically.

With the theme in the back of my mind, I go outdoors. I love hiking, mountain biking, and bodyboarding. So today, as the wind is good, I bring out my kite and go for a stroll down to the beachfront. As I yank on the handles and the kite goes soaring into the sky, my problems are whisked away into the air with it. As I pull to the left the kite drops like a bird. As I pull to the right, I feel it climb back up to the clouds. It's just good old-fashioned fun. And as I do this, the theme of "light and dark" is going around in my head.

I think the first part of my concept development is making sure that I am on the right track. I feel since the theme is so broad, that working backwards will help me come to a visual repertoire of elements to work with. I try to think of what will not work. Translucent or nearly transparent forms such as glass or water will contain light and dark areas, but I just don't think they will give that "hitting the nail right on the head" sort of message. I want a solid object to work with, something that emphasizes areas of light, and shadows. I need this visual translation of the subject to be bold and obvious. Rather than being conceptual, the final artwork simply has to work, no questions asked.

The light and dark theme could utilize anything for its object, as without light and shade there would be no form. I think of an apple, hanging from its branch, swaying from side to side, dappled with moving shadows as the light filters through the leaves.

This theme is so broad, that I could have used an apple. But because I have decided that any object or form could be used, this made room for inspirational subject matter.

To me, nothing is more inspirational than architecture. I feel that architects are the true artists, visualizing, sketching and building their solutions. A good friend named Benjamin O'Meara was one of the most talented creative thinkers that I have had the honor of meeting. With a background in architecture, his style was raw and free from contamination. His work was an inspiration.

Because the 'light and dark' subject matter could be so broad, I confined it to architecture. The images used in this series were shot in Laguna Beach California, where I live. There is a small uprising of good architecture along the crest of the "Top of the World" recreational park. I feel these buildings are the perfect subject matter to exemplify light and dark. Their geometric shapes rely on light and contrasting shadow for their visual impact, and on a sunny afternoon here in Southern California, the forms just come to life. As I was shooting the homes people would walk by wondering what I was doing and why. But, I proceeded with my photography. I was curious about the people living within. The walls seemed to be covered with abstract and modern art. Every home seemed to have a telescope to gaze upon their 360-degree mountain-top view. And each of them seemed to have a Lincoln Navigator with a matching Ferrari 360 Moderna in the driveway. Maybe one day one of them will invite me in for a cup of coffee.

I was pleased when I viewed the imagery. There were a number of images to choose from, and the ones chosen for the pieces were the best suited for the job, with angles and lines that I thought would compliment each other.

As I work on a piece, there are no speed bumps. It's just a few hours of strolling experimentation before I come up with something new. There is no definitive process as to how I reach this point. In Photoshop I can create a piece with anything from 4 to 40 layers. Every time, it seems to be different. The overall aesthetic manner of the piece may link to my past work, but I try to have my work evolve to become new and different.

My main goal with this project was to show high contrast imagery juxtaposed with low contrast imagery. The light blue piece is a soft approach to form. It is as if the piece is as light as a feather. The darker piece of the two is to bluntly expose the lights and darks of the form. The overlayed imagery is to add essence and accent to the piece, as the background imagery gives body.

I feel that I am beginning to move into another realm with my work. I have worked with imagery for years now, and I feel it is time to move into another medium. Type has always interested me, but I have never fully immersed myself in experimentation with it. So I feel this will be my next direction. Also, thanks to the Internet, I am eager to get into some new user interface designs. I would like to transfer classic layout techniques and canvas composition to the Internet. After all, everything is design.

I feel that if I can work every corner of the design spectrum, I can become a successful designer. By this I mean working with imagery, artwork, type, and motion, involving all these elements without fear and working well with them. I use my website as a place where I can post my latest endeavors with experimental layouts and solutions, and get some feedback. People write me most expressing curiosity on how I developed certain imagery, and it's always my pleasure to strike up a conversation with them. In the future I hope to dedicate more time to the site. I have had various concepts brewing in the back of my head for quite some time now, that I'd like to follow up. In particular I'd like to learn more about 3D, something I know little about at the moment. I've got this idea about a 3D insect type thing that could be used as an interactive vehicle for portraying images of my memories. This is obviously at a very embryonic stage, but all the possibilities out there still to be explored excite me and keep me doing what I do.

© 2000 The Designers Republic Ltd.

©www.one9ine.com

©Arnaud Mercier www.elixirstudio.com

As a designer always seeking refuge from the obvious route of design problem solving, I've always been fond of the work done by The Designers Republic. (www.thedesignersrepublic.com) In an interview at http://shift.jp.org/ (articles archive) the founder of the Designers Republic, Ian Anderson, notes that their design solutions do not mirror or reflect any other past or current design solutions. He sees himself and the guys he works with as designers who are filters for their own experiences, not other people's creativity, and credits this with their success. With this said, it is difficult not to absorb what is seen in your surroundings. For instance if you were to look at any magazine you would be instantly bombarded with a myriad of designs, some successful, some less so. When you get back to work at your computer terminal, it's up to you to filter that experience. If you do not have the self-discipline and imagination to find a new and original route, you are spelling your own downfall as a creative new media designer.

Another inspiration of mine is Matt Owens of http://one9ine.com He has successfully progressed, leaving behind a trail of successful design solutions. He leads an inspirational lifestyle that any designer would advocate – that of being a freelance artist. It's the only way to live.

Arnaud Mercier of http://www.elixirstudio.com has also been an inspiration to me. Arnaud has always approached his solutions by thinking outside the box. This always seems to produce successful and aesthetically pleasing results. There are no weak points in his work. From motion graphics to still imagery, every frame is a pleasure to view.

Bareback: The Tomato Project has always been a favorite book in my collection. The work seems to be created from personal phenomena and occurrences rather than implemented designs and vigorously thought out arrangements. It's more of a scrapbook of thoughts and ideas. Also the book *soakwashrinsespin* by the Tolleson Design Group has been a good asset when referring to a professional assessment of how to go about the process of branding. Their presentation of the solution is phenomenal.

I'm also influenced by many other academic areas, besides art. During my studies I was disciplined in many areas of mathematics, philosophy and aesthetics. Thanks to my time dedicated to these subject matters in the past, I am now able to formulate an educated response to my design problems.

This was done for http://shift.jp.org/ in the year 2000. This marked the beginning of using my own personal photography. After spending a few weeks hunting for the perfect lighting conditions and subject matter, I came up with this great shot. One key necessity in this shot was to have the flower dropping from the ceiling of the browser window. Also, because I wanted natural lighting, I had to endure the elements that came with the outdoors. After my first photo shoot a storm passed through and lasted for three days. I learned a whole lot from this project.

This piece was created in response to the title "Interactive Digital Media: The New Literacy", (see Gary Birch, http://www.statmedia.com). As an exercise, individual designers were asked to create around this theme. In doing so, I made several breakthroughs in my work. These included morphing imagery, sensitivity of audio, gestalt movement, and simplicity of navigation.

gital media... the new literacy

os theory- winter

This was a piece created for http://www.kiiroi.nu in a collaboration effort with http://www.loopehole8.com of Turkey. This broadened my range of influence from Southern California to worldwide overnight. It was definitely a pleasure working with my partner on this project, and we were up against Mike Young of http://www.designgraphik.com. The project was to visually describe winter.

Both teams came up with radically different solutions, that were both out of the ordinary. It was a blast.

I love the possibilities that collaboration can offer, and that's why the concept behind this book is so exciting. As I completed my first two pieces I was eager to begin work on another designers canvas. And as eager as I was to experience another working environment, I was anxious to have another look into my own. It's as if this is a validating process. We will discover if our solutions are worthy of being labeled as successful. To create something that is aesthetically pleasing is easy. To create something functional is simple. But to create an aesthetically pleasing vehicle that fulfils its ordained purpose is a challenge. One of my goals when creating for this theme was to give priority to producing something that was an inspiration to others, putting this before aesthetic goals. If I can retain this order the work will be successful. You may find that you will run into trouble if the aesthetics come before the function.

The body of work within this book could offer a change in the art world. In any large city you can find art galleries full of artwork created by one person. But imagine how rich that artwork could become if it were exposed to the ideas of another artist? Do you know how it feels when you're looking for a movie, but nothing really seems to appeal? It's not that there aren't any good movies there, but it's the fact that movie A offers B, and movie C offers D. But no movie can offer all of the elements you are looking for. If we could take our artwork, and hand it over to another designer, the work has the potential of becoming phenomenal! I am very excited to see where my work will go, and what I can contribute to the works of the other designers at hand.

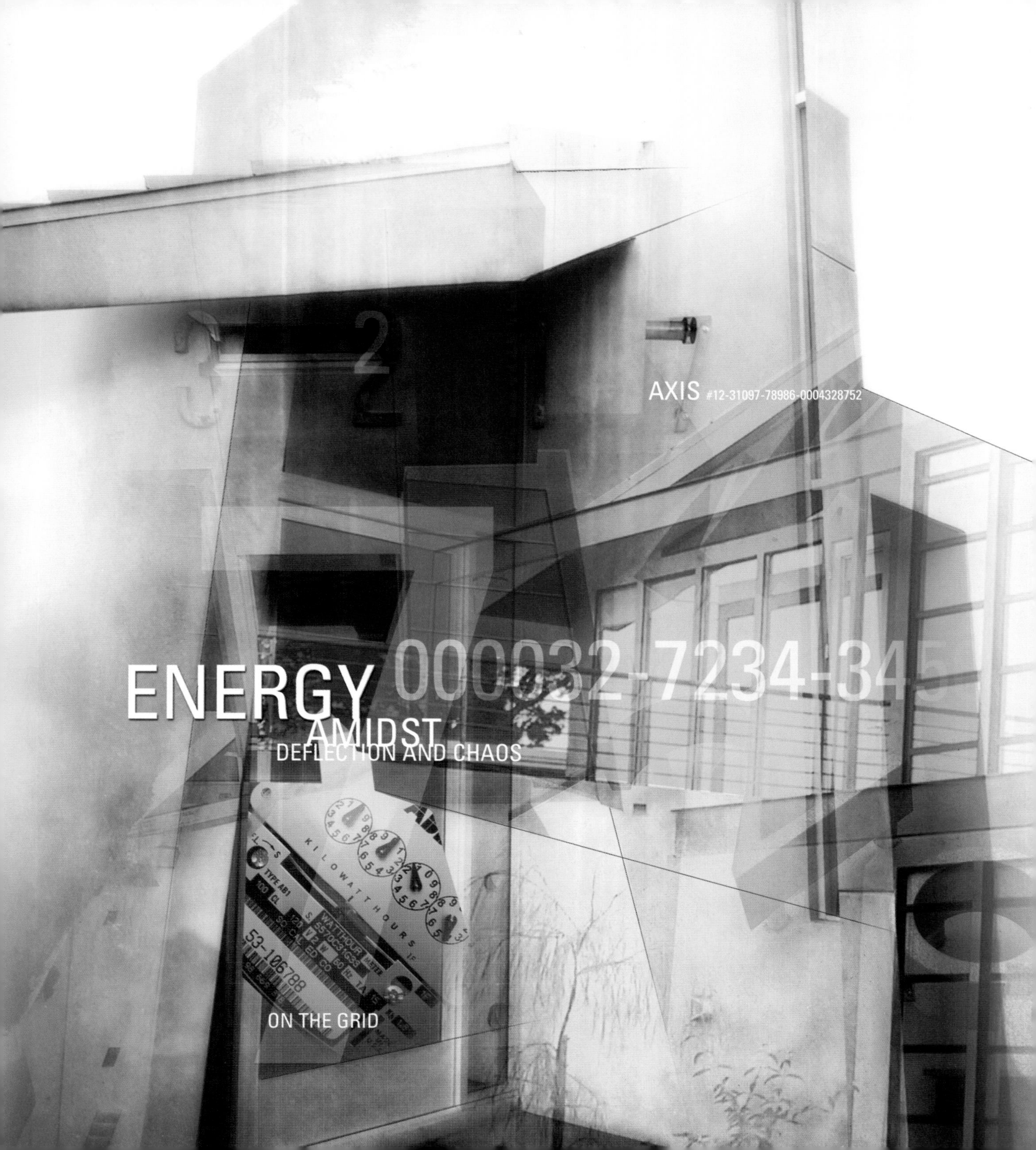
AXIS #12-31097-78986-0004328752
ENERGY 000032-7234-345
AMIDST
DEFLECTION AND CHAOS
ON THE GRID
KILOWATTHOURS

ON THE GRID

TRANSLUCENCE

SHADOW

SURFACE

TRANSLUCENCE

CAST

The human thought process is complex and pretty difficult to decipher. At times even deciding between two t-shirts in the mini mall can be a task. Our brains have the capacity to reach a conclusion on this kind of decision, but when it comes to thought processes there really is no structure for us to rely upon. Trying to explain how the decision was eventually reached can be tricky.

I was told during my studies that upon commencing a project I should go through a strenuous process of brainstorming and thumbnail sketching in order to filter out any bad ideas. "This," my betters told me, "will produce the perfect solution!" The word I have a problem with here is 'perfect'. You could go through your entire working life and never have a perfect day. You arrive at the studio late from time to time. You might just spill a little tea on your tie. And every day is different, isn't it? Instead of seeking a perfect day, I suggest letting go and allowing the day to take you for a ride. See what happens and smile as you experience events unfolding.

Many of my colleagues have asked about my thought process for problem solving within my creative work. Most might expect complex theories and deeply thought out methods, but the truth is that there is no structured thought process. If I try and go through routine alpha and beta phases of creative development I lose interest. This isn't boredom with the work itself, but with the thought process responsible for its production. It's bland and regular, with no experimentation, ambiguity or surprise to spice things up.

On a daily basis I go running through rough terrain in my local mountains. It's exciting and there is high potential for danger. To help you understand my reasoning behind blowing out structured creative thought processes, and rigid working methods, I would like you to imagine you are a mountain runner. Think about going along the same trail over and over again, day in and day out. It will become boring after a few weeks. You can rock that trail inside and out, and hit the inclines at a solid pace, because you know the route like the back of your hand. This may be good for strength training, but will you excel as a runner if you never experience the challenges that other trails may offer? In order to develop, you have to try out those other trails. In doing so you may feel a little disoriented at first, there may be risks involved and you may trip or fall occasionally, but once you make it to the top of one mountain there's nothing that can prevent you from climbing all the others in the area. In other words, experimentation is good for growth.

Much can be gained in design and fine art by letting go of previously learned methods and structures. This is what you are seeing here in this tutorial. I am devoting this work to freestyle methods without boundaries or structure. These methods include experimenting with various elements that I would not normally use and attempting new tricks, with the aim of introducing more variety into my work.

It's not often, outside my website, that I am able to share this experimental method with the world, so please take this opportunity to move it into your style of thinking. It just might change how you see things.

1_master.psd

Thankfully, I have a wealth of good imagery from my architecture photo shoot. All I have to do get the piece underway is to find an image that will be a strong base for any future overlaid components.

First I created a new canvas, 8 x 9 inches tall, with a resolution of 300 dpi. This will become my playground. At this moment I feel pure excitement, no tension, because there is very little that can wrong from this point. When doing experimental work, it's all about going freestyle and seeing what happens.

1_a.jpg

Image 1_a.jpg is very strong. The composition is harmonious and the overall balance between light and dark is nearly perfect. Detail can be seen in the shadowed areas of the image. This is a rule of thumb for good photography. If the image is too dark in the shadowed areas, the exposure setting on your camera may be too high. It's best to get a well-balanced raw image first, and move into high contrast in Photoshop later.

First I dragged image 1_a.jpg into my canvas. I arranged the image to the composition that I wanted by resizing it using Edit > Transform > Scale, so that it fills the canvas height-wise without distorting it too much. (Note that all my source images are rectangular whereas the canvas is nearly square, so this is not an exact science, rather do what you think looks good.)

I have found that it is easier to work without color when manipulating complex imagery. If the images are left in full hue problems, may arise from over-saturation and posterization. Using shades of gray, there is only one tone to work with, and this simplifies the problem-solving process. This in turn minimizes image complexity. I will add hue to the piece when it is nearer completion.

I proceeded to desaturate the image, using Image > Adjust > Desaturate (shift + cmd + u / shift + ctrl + u). You could just put it into grayscale before bringing it in, but I always like to leave myself the option of bringing the original color back.

I then decided I wanted to clean up the image a little. A few details, such as the bush, the light switch and the door handle, make it a little too busy, which I feel detracts from the overall impression. After all, this is our base. There's plenty more detail to come! (I usually zoom in and use the clone option on the Rubber Stamp tool to do this kind of job.) I also removed the right-hand part of the picture where the wall comes in and obscures the window, as this was the only bit of the composition of the photo I wasn't so keen on. I used the Polygonal Lasso tool to make a selection, and then deleted the selected area.

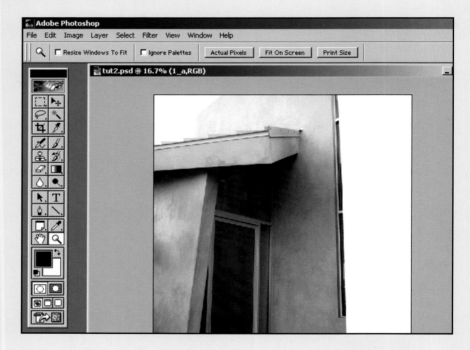

Because I knew that I would be overlaying multiple images on top of layer 1_a, I decided to use a technique I've developed that softens the large surfaces of photographs, while preserving the contrasting edges in the image.

First I created a copy of the image layer, and with that layer selected, went into Filter > Blur > Gaussian Blur, setting the radius at 10 pixels. Next I lowered the opacity of the new layer to 30% by adjusting the opacity slider in the layers palette. At this point you can see the benefits of using this technique. There is almost a glow or halo effect that happens, but in all the right areas. Edges are softened, but their clarity is not. It's awesome!

1_e.jpg

On the right hand side of the image, there is a blank area of canvas. At first I felt that this area might be a problem, but after a little consideration I realized it would be easy to find something that would work here. I noticed a surface in another image from this shoot that may be of some assistance here. *Image 1_e.jpg* was dragged and dropped into the canvas, and again I went through the process of resizing and moving it until I was happy with the way the two images fitted together. (I find it helps to drop the opacity of the new layer down to about 30% temporarily so that you can get a good idea of how the part of the new image you want will fit in before you cut it.) Then I desaturated it, as before, and restored its opacity.

Hiding layer 1_e in the Layers palette so I could see what I was doing easily, I selected the blank area in layer 1_a with the Magic Wand tool (set to a low tolerance number), and inverted the selection (cmd + shift + I / ctrl + shift + I). Then I clicked on layer 1_e to select it in the Layers palette, and deleted the selected area, as I felt this part did not compliment the composition, and I really only wanted the bit on the right to fill the gap.

In order to avoid jagged edges when deleting a selection in imagery, I suggest setting the selection to feather at 2 pixels, using Select > Feather (option + cmd + d / alt + ctrl + d) to bring up the dialog box. Now when you delete you will have a nice soft feather on your selected area.

To be honest, I think I have been lucky with this image on the right side – it's from a totally different structure all together, and the image balance is almost identical to the image it is merged with. I cleaned up the image a bit, removing a few details such as the tree to the right. I think I'm pretty happy with this so far.

1_b.jpg

Image *1_b.jpg* is another strong image. And to my delight, as I dragged and dropped this image onto my canvas and set the layer blend mode to Overlay, all of the light areas were banished leaving the dark area's impression on the underlying images. This happy circumstance prompted me to move and adjusted the image to work in harmony with the images around it. Composition in my work deals with rules from time to time, but in creative work it's largely a matter of taste. I suggest you play around with your images, until they look right together.

As for myself, I rotated it about 90 degrees clockwise, and scaled it up using Edit > Free Transform. I wanted to keep the chimney to the right of the porch in layer 1_a, so I stopped scaling when that was where I wanted it, and when the composition felt right.

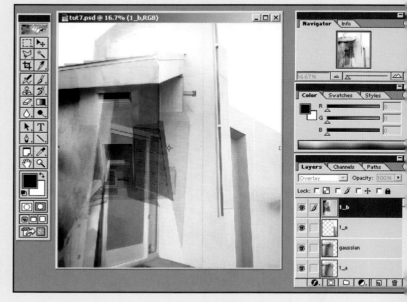

1_c.jpg

Image *1_c.jpg* is a cool one. It's actually the beginning of a mailbox for one of these awesome modern homes. The numbers were made of heavy brass in order to achieve an intentional dripping effect in the morning dew. It reminds me of that cool technique of mixing turpentine into your oil paints in fine art. It makes your work aesthetically curious and disturbing.

Anyhow, I felt it was time to add a little type to the piece. Not type in the sense of Photoshop type, but 3-dimensional type from the real world. I simply dragged and dropped the image onto the canvas, desaturated it, and set the blend mode to Overlay in the Layers palette. Then I stretched it vertically and horizontally through Transform, until I got the composition I wanted.

1_d.jpg

To add a bit of curiosity to the piece I decided to throw in the complex image of an energy meter. I usually try to avoid loud, hectic images like this but because I wanted to challenge my normal approach to this piece I decided to throw it in and take it for a test drive. Anyhow, if the image didn't work how I wanted, the Layer Delete button was only a click away...

After a bit of playing with the composition of the image, I found a home for it. I rotated the image about 45 degrees clockwise and scaled it down using the free transform function, Edit > Free Transform (cmd + T / ctrl + T). After setting the Layer Blend mode to Overlay, I noticed a strong hold coming from the background images (*1_a.jpg* and *1_b.jpg*), particularly the triangular shadow at the bottom left of the door, and the angular shapes of 1_b across the center of the door in 1_a.

Once again this was a welcome surprise that opened the way for some more experimentation. I selected the area of the meter image that was surrounded by these strong image parts using the Polygonal Lasso tool then inverted the selection and deleted the edges.

I desaturated the image. Now the effect coming through from the background images was even more accentuated!

1_g.jpg and 1_f.jpg

Because I had already added some 3-dimensional type elements to the piece, I figured a few more wouldn't look out of place. Here all I did was drag and drop the images into the canvas and set them to Overlay.

At the sight of any hard edges (say, where layers had been noticeably overlayed) I used the Eraser set to airbrush at 150 pixels to eliminate these edges. These can be dangerous, adding too much information to the finished piece. Just select the layer in the Layers palette and click away.

Of course, if you need to, create a new brush. Click the arrow on the top right of the drop-down brush menu, go to new brush, diameter 150, hardness 1, spacing checked at 25%.

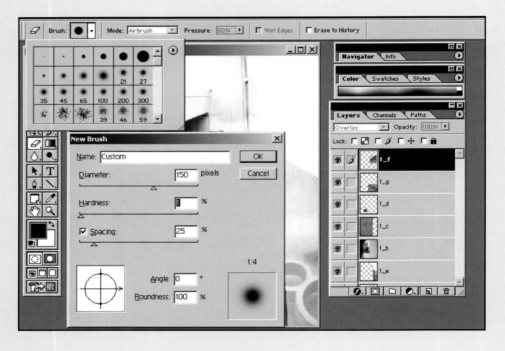

To add some flavor to this area of the canvas, I decided not to desaturate these images – we'll just have to see what that does for us later on!

1_h.jpg

Complexity in form is chaos harnessed. Look at all the beautiful edges and lines in image *1_h.jpg*. This image is splendid. I proceeded to drag this image to my canvas and set it to Overlay.

Now, because this image is so strong, and brings in so much complexity in contrast to our smooth background images, I have decided to cut out the background information in order to harness this beast. At this point I located a focal point within my canvas. It is from here that the eye will move throughout the composition. With a little adjustment, I find its placement (towards the center of the piece) and select the area I would like to keep in the image, invert the selection, and delete.

Also, to add a bit of surprise I decided not to desaturate this image. I wanted to see what kind of color combination I could get when I did my color burns later on in the process.

Edge gradients

It is not totally necessary, but I added some gradients to the edge of the canvas. I noticed the canvas was becoming a little unbalanced thanks to the harsh shadow on the left side. For fun, I added this white gradient that mixed well with the sky above. I used the Rectangular Marquee tool to select the left hand edge of the canvas, to about an inch and a half in. Then I used a white to transparent gradient coming in from the left. It's a bit confusing to look at for the first time, but soon after your eyes become settled, you might just like what you see. Again to balance what I have done on the left side of the canvas, I have added a gradient to the right hand side as well. I feel this accentuates the gaussian halo technique described in setting up the background *1_a*.

Soft light hue additions

Ah... at last, color addition. After working the piece a bit with minor tweaks here and there, I feel it is complete in terms of imagery and overlaying techniques. Because the imagery in the background for the most part is desaturated, any swatch that I select will add hue to the form. On a new layer I simply select a color from the Swatch palette and using the Paint Bucket fill the layer with the hue. (I have chosen a mid-blue.) Now with the layer full of color I set the layer blend mode to Soft Light. Color Burn or Overlay will not work to give this type of effect. Color Burn I find is very harsh and somewhat posterizes images at 100%. Overlay is strong and adds high contrast to the image. And Soft Light is a lighter version of Overlay.

I have duplicated the Soft Light layer in order to achieve better control of percentage combination of the Soft Light option. By doing this you can get a higher degree of color saturation in your image without it being as harsh as Color burn or Overlay.

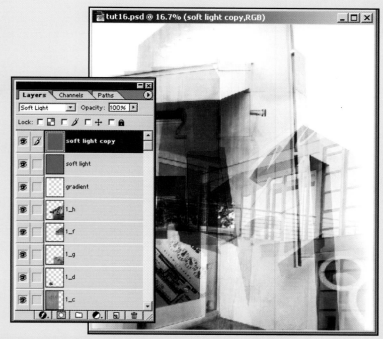

Highlighting

In order to highlight the focal point even more, I used the Polygonal Lasso tool to select any areas I felt were interesting and defined the overall structure of the background imagery. Next I created a new layer and filled it with a mid-blue color selected from the Swatch palette. I set this to Soft Light.

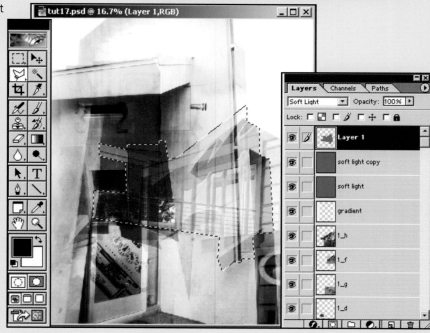

Lines

To accentuate any areas that add rigidity to the piece, I highlighted with the Line tool, using the Create Filled Region option on the toolbar with the options set to 1 pixel stroke, anti-alias activated. I highlighted any areas that I felt were strong edges in the piece, and accentuated its focal point. If I were to select this area with the Marquee tool, invert the selection and delete the outside areas of the canvas, I feel the piece would still be strong.

Grid

To add some flavor to the piece, I added a grid taken from a screenshot of Illustrator with the background grid activated (grid.jpg). I took the screenshot and opened it in Photoshop. Then I selected, dragged and dropped the grid into my working canvas, enlarged it using Transform, inverted the image to become black, and set the layer to screen. This gives me the white lines from the grid while screening the black areas of the screenshot.

Type

As mentioned earlier, there is a visual focal point or hub within the piece that the eye is drawn to. This constitutes the visual gestalt. Let me explain.

As someone looks at a new subject matter, in this case a design, it begins to travel. Generally speaking the eye does not feel comfortable focusing on one point for longer than five or six seconds at a time. In order to prevent the viewer losing interest, and to make your canvas less flat and more interesting, you can put the gestalt principle to use. Strong focal points in the piece are areas where lines meet and where hues darken.

For instance, if I were looking at an apple, a strong focal point would be where the base of the stem meets the top of the apple. By selecting and highlighting strong focal points, I can create a piece that will compliment the eye's natural desire to explore and move round the canvas. One way of accentuating these points is by using text.

The phrases and lines of text I've used are a brainstorm on the theme of *Light & Dark*, and the imagery that I've used. My hope is that they encourage viewers to engage with the piece, and that they add to the wonder of its exploration.

For this demonstration I chose to use the Univers font. This is not a standard Photoshop or system font, neither is it freeware, so unfortunately if you want it you have to buy it. It is a modern sans-serif font that can be used for electronic projects, layout or print. It's one of my personal favorites, but any other sans-serif font, (one where the angled edges of the characters have no tails) could be used to similar effect.

In keeping with the 'light' feeling I'm trying to create with this piece, I used white text. I wanted the numbers to be more part of the general design than something a viewer would actually read, so I varied the size and opacity until I felt they were an addition rather than an intrusion. I wanted the words to have more of an impact, so I left their opacity at 100%, and added a drop shadow effect to the most important text, ENERGY. (Layer > Layer Style > Drop Shadow, settings as below)

As with everything else in this piece, my recommendation is for you to experiment with these techniques, until you find something you like.

Here's what the final file should look like:

2_master.psd

In an attempt to employ variety amongst my imagery, I have taken the overall tone of *2_master.psd* to a darker and fuller level. In this piece I used a few methods that I have never tried out before and a color scheme that I have never used until now. Let's see how it was created.

2_a.jpg

This image is awesome! I knew it would be, even as I was taking the photograph. I'm not used to working in this near square format, so most of the imagery I have is rectangular. In order to use the imagery captured I usually have to either expand the image to flood the canvas area or use a different image to fill the white gap left behind by the narrow image. I enlarged it, using Edit > Transform > Scale, but left it rectangular so that I did not lose the information in the outer edges of the image.

I decided on attempting something new to solve the problem of the gap on the right hand side of the canvas. I created a duplicate of the layer and proceeded to flip it horizontally, using Edit > Transform > Flip Horizontal.

The result is a seamless solution to the image gap at hand. If there were a lot of recognizable objects in the area where the seam was merged, I could run into trouble. But thankfully, everything is looking good.

2_b.jpg

2_b.jpg is a shot of one of my favorite homes. It was backlit as the sun was going down, so you can see the light coming through the front door. Here I opened the image in Photoshop and dragged and dropped the image into a new layer in my main canvas. I set the Layer Blend mode to overlay, and resized it using Edit > Transform > Scale, again preserving its original shape.

I duplicated the layer and flipped it vertically this time.

Note: in *1_master.psd* I desaturated most of my layers due to image complexity and posterization. As I go through this process without desaturating the images, watch how the canvas slowly becomes darker and more difficult to read. This is a cool effect if you are attempting to provoke a deeper, darker emotional response from your audience.

2_c.jpg

This image is actually shot out of the context of this architectural shoot. I didn't want to stay too close to home on this one, so I ventured out and found a structure that offered a dynamic crossbar section. This in turn would add a perspective feel to my piece, while preserving the wealth of the original background images.

The coolest thing about Overlay is that it simply accentuates the background image without taking from it. Here I opened the image in Photoshop, dragged and dropped the image to a new layer, and set the image to Overlay. I rotated it 90 degrees clockwise, using Edit > Transform > Rotate, then resized it, using Edit > Transform > Scale. I moved it around and played with it until I was happy with the composition of the piece.

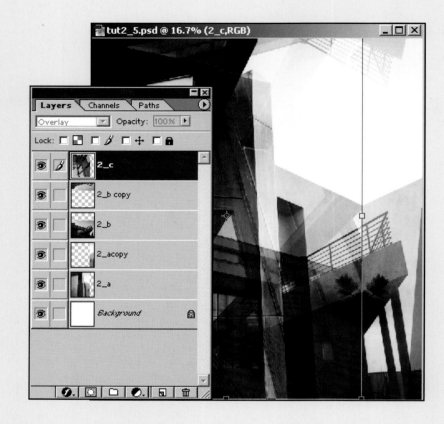

I then removed a few debris that I felt did not compliment the overall composition of the piece, using the Eraser tool set to airbrush at 150, hardness 1, spacing checked at 25%. A light semi-circular area in the top right of the piece was lessening the impact of the reflection of the railings, and there were some lines and a beam in the bottom right quarter that I felt would be better removed.

Black overlay

To give this piece a darker feel, I created a new layer, used the Paint Bucket to fill it with black, and set the layer blend mode to Overlay. I reduced the opacity to 10%, as although I wanted to darken the piece as a whole, I didn't want to lose all the detail in the shadowed areas.

Complementary hue

Because the overall tint of the piece at this moment is blue, I thought I would add a complementary hue to the piece. I wanted the master images, when juxtaposed, to represent the polarity of the light and dark theme, and so I thought I would use red to add a warmth that would contrast with the light blue coldness of the first piece. After creating a new layer and filling it with red, I set the Layer Effect to Overlay and lowered the opacity to 50%.

Type

Once again, I decided to add type layers to give the piece a more definite title, here the solid feel of 'Form and Function' contrasting with the theme of energy I used for the 'light' piece.

Sometimes I am very literal with how I approach my work. If I were to approach every canvas with the same formula of naming conventions, the work might lose its curiosity and innocence. In mixing it up, there are always new possibilities.

In piece 2 I have scattered text that defines the particular focal point. The phrase 'shadow' is overlapping the area that's in shadow. In another area of the piece I have written 'translucence'. This text overlaps an area that is translucent.

Once again I used Univers, but as mentioned before any sans-serif font will give a similar effect, just play around until you find one you like.

The colors were taken using the Eyedropper tool, rather than just picking out a color, as this ensures that your choice fits in with the piece as a whole.

To achieve transparency with high contrast, on the number 1 and the 'form and function' text, I used white text and set the layer blend mode to Overlay.

Finally, remember that text is just like any other element – it can be enlarged, rotated and moved around. My method of working is to play around with the composition of various elements until I reach a point where I'm happy with the piece.

I used to sit in my bedroom when I was a kid with the lights low, listening to heavy metal, copying Iron Maiden album covers. Derek Riggs was a hero (he's the guy who did all of the cover illustrations of the mythical *Eddie*). Yeah, I think my mother worried about that. Skulls, devils, pitchforks and loud music in a dark room. What was fascinating to me about Maiden though was this amazing imagery their music created, it was almost like reading some kind of strange history book. Tales of ancient worlds, of historical figures and great wars, more fiction than fact. It was storytelling. Oh how easy it is to capture the imagination of eleven year old boy!

Things haven't changed much in the last fifteen years. I sit in my living room with the lights low, listening to heavy metal, but now I'm creating my own work and trying to tell my own stories. My stuff is always very personal. Almost every project on goingonsix.com is about a person in my life. A friend, a brother, a sister, a lover. Some of the projects are more fiction than fact and some are taken straight out of conversations and very real situations. My work in the past, when I was at college, was similar but more focused on trying to figure myself out - what I liked and disliked, what I reacted to and felt strongly about. Nothing was ever worth creating if I couldn't put myself into it somehow. There always had to be meaning. I wanted to be able to look back on the things I had made and say, "Yeah, that's where my head was at." That's probably why I still work in my free time. It's like my journal.

A YEAR OF RECKONING.

01.THE DIVER 02.POSTCARDS TO HOME 03.UNTITLED.01 04.SCRAPYARD 05.SIXSCREENS (WALLPAPERS)
06.BREAKOUT (BY NATZKE) 07.SIMPLE FASCINATIONS 08.MY X-FILES 09.WHISPERING 10.EXCERPTS FROM A BROKEN HEART
11.ZIGG ZAGG 12.OUR TECHNOLOGIES 13.THE PROS AND CONS 14.46&2 15.THEYETI@GOINGONSIX.COM

1993

3

Oddly enough, I never really used a computer till my sophomore year in college at the age of eighteen. I think I might have had one computer class in high school. I cheated my way through it because I simply had no interest. My freshman year of college at the School of Visual Arts was foundation year classes: painting, drawing, sculpture, photography, and so on... When I was growing up my parents could never afford a computer and truth be told I probably wouldn't have used it anyway. I was into freestyle BMX bikes and playing ice hockey – no way would I have sat inside on a sunny day messing around on one of those things. A lot of my designer pals are into video games, but I'm not really into those either. I liked *Mike Tyson's Punch Out* and *Nintendo Ice Hockey* with the skinny guy, the medium guy and the fat guy but aside from that they've always just kind of bored me. Anyway, my sophomore year of college was the first time I really sat down and messed with anything. I had this one class where we used Superpaint to make some funky shapes and patterns and in the second half of the class we graduated to the ever-elusive Photoshop. I think I started with version 2. Man – did the type tool ever suck in version 2! I forget what the theme of the project was but I used Photoshop for scanning sketches and photos and then actually putting them together in a composition. We then printed the comps through a blueprint printer and painted on them or did further drawing. This was so amazing to me because I never realized that a computer could be an integral part of a much larger process. This is where I fell in love. Photoshop was this new powerful tool that opened up new ways for me to think about the work I was creating. For me though, Photoshop is no more important than a litho press or a paintbrush or a pencil and I think that's a good thing to always keep in mind. Well, it's a good thing to keep in mind but I have to be honest and say I use Photoshop way more than litho presses and paintbrushes!

WE'RE LIKE APPLES
AND ORANGES.

So getting back to Maiden... music's always played a big role in my world. My CD collection is like the soundtrack to the movie that is my life and I can't work without it.   Mom and Dad always had some vinyl spinning. When I was like twelve or thirteen I got into a debate with my father about music. He insisted that none of the bands I listened to were heavier than the bands he listened to, and demonstrated this by throwing on some Jethro Tull. I remember saying to myself, "Man, this is pretty heavy." I wasn't sure what to do, but I had to top him. So I put on *Last Caress/Green Hell* from Metallica's *Garage Days Re-Revisited*. He shrugged it off, laughed even. He said, "This ain't shit son!" and put something else on. I can't remember what it was right now, but it was on the level. So the battle was on! I was determined. I unlocked my dresser drawer (this was where I put stuff I didn't want my Mother to find) and pulled out... Slayer. That's right, Slayer! I believe it was the album *Hell Awaits*. With a look of pride and spite smeared across my face I slapped that tape in and hit play. "Victory is mine!" I thought. But when I looked up at my parents all I remember seeing was this look of utter disgust, shock and horror. It took my mother about 20 seconds and she'd had enough. "What the hell is this crap? Let me see the case!" Needless to say the flying hell demons on the cover and a song called *Kill Again* didn't sit too well. I think they were a little scared of me after that but they never did take those Slayer tapes away. I guess the moral here is that I grew up on some great music with some pretty understanding and patient parents and I thank them for that.

When it comes to more traditional influences, namely artists and designers, I like to think I'm still in a constant state of discovery and rediscovery. At this point it's only appropriate to say a big thank you to my freshman year painting instructor Farrell Brickhouse. This guy had more energy, love and passion for what he created and taught then anyone I'd ever met before or since for that matter. He turned me on to painters I'd never heard of before. He'd see things in your work and say, "Have you ever seen this guy's stuff?" You'd say no and he'd show up the next day with a book breaking down intricacies and showing you why this worked and that didn't. I could go on and on. My favorite painter is Francis Bacon, who, some would argue, is one of the greatest figure painters the world has ever seen. I'd have to agree. Not only was he capable of capturing the human form in his most unique and expressive way but also seemed able to capture something of the human spirit. Robert Rauschenberg, David Salle, Cy Twombly and Chuck Close, all amazing, work I'll always look to for inspiration or to just simply blow my mind. Color, shape, texture, photography, type, grids - the masters know how to use it all.

I've been inspired by a load of graphic designers, from Moholy-Nagy to Carson. A Muller-Brockmann ad for Hermes Typewriters or a Dirk Rudolph album cover for Rammstein, it's all important to me. More than anything I think I'm just a fan who's lucky enough to participate in my own little way. Jemma Gura got me into Ed Ruscha who I'd never heard of before. Is he an artist or a designer? Juxtaposed found words painted on canvas. Backdrops of mountains or wood grain. I'm not sure. I think graphic design is a very broad term for so many different things. More and more I think the lines between art and design are blurred and the more they're blurred the more people seem to explore tradition and fundamentals to maybe bring back some perspective. The web is a good place to explore all of these things though. Personal web space is important to try new things, explore ideas and technique, give them a place to sit and let them grow on you. Otherwise, you're doing the client thing all the time. Helping sell furniture or someone's album or Barbie dolls or... It's all what you make it out to be. There's so much out there, so much saturation, you just kind of have to take it all in, process and personalize, figure out what turns you on. There are so many people doing so much great work. On the web, in print, in broadcast. I try to keep up, it's hard, but I try and take something from all these different mediums just so I never stop learning.

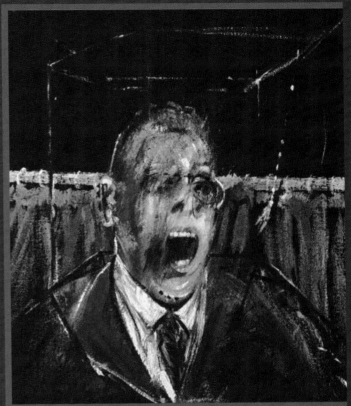

Study for a Portrait by Francis Bacon
© Christie's Images/CORBIS

Another big influence for me was, and still is, graffiti. When I was about nine or ten my grandfather took me on the subway for the first time. It was early in the morning, we were standing on the platform, the train pulled in and the car that stopped in front of us had been painted the night before, top to bottom, by Futura 2000. It was one of the most amazing things I had ever seen. The colors, the letters, the characters, the sheer scale of the piece. From that day on I was hooked. I dabbled on paper here and there, obsessed over the book *Subway Art* and went as far as spray painting and airbrushing my bedroom walls (my father wasn't thrilled about this but I think he understood). When I got to high school, I met a couple of guys who were just as into it and a whole lot better than me. We would draw together all the time and pass black books (sketchbooks) back and forth. When I open that old book now I could say to myself, "Man, you sucked", but it's not about that. It's about being able to look back to see where my head was at. It's about being able to take something from those old sketches and ideas, remove them from their original context and re-purpose them for something new and fresh. I learned a lot from them and this experience. I still have one of the books and I recently paid homage to it in a piece called *The System*. There's always a theme or a story, it's rooted in something tangible (the book itself) and something intangible (the memories I have of doing this stuff with my friends). This idea is a recurring theme in my work. Trying to find a link between images and memories, and creating stories out of them.

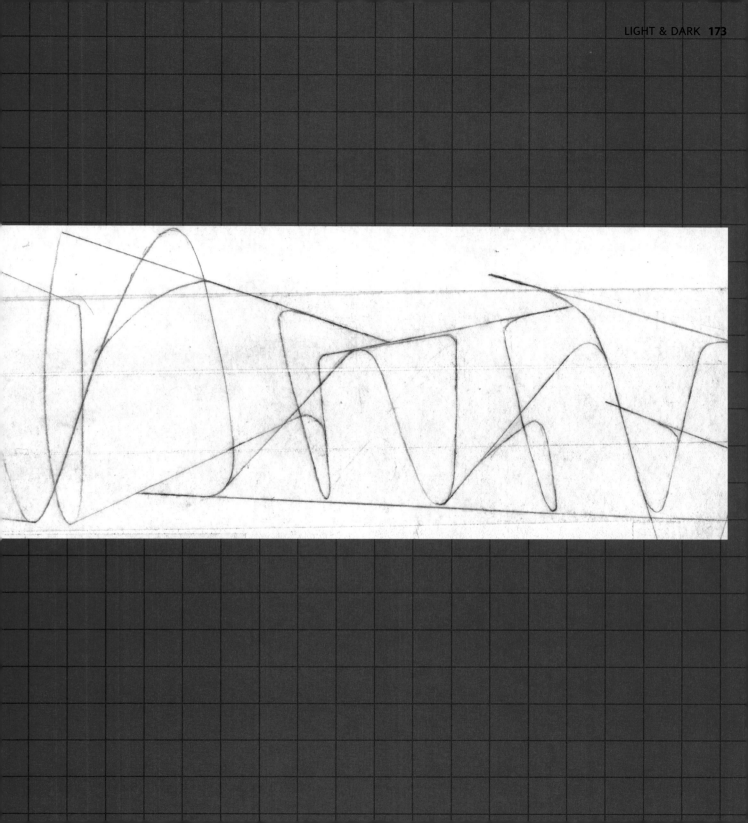

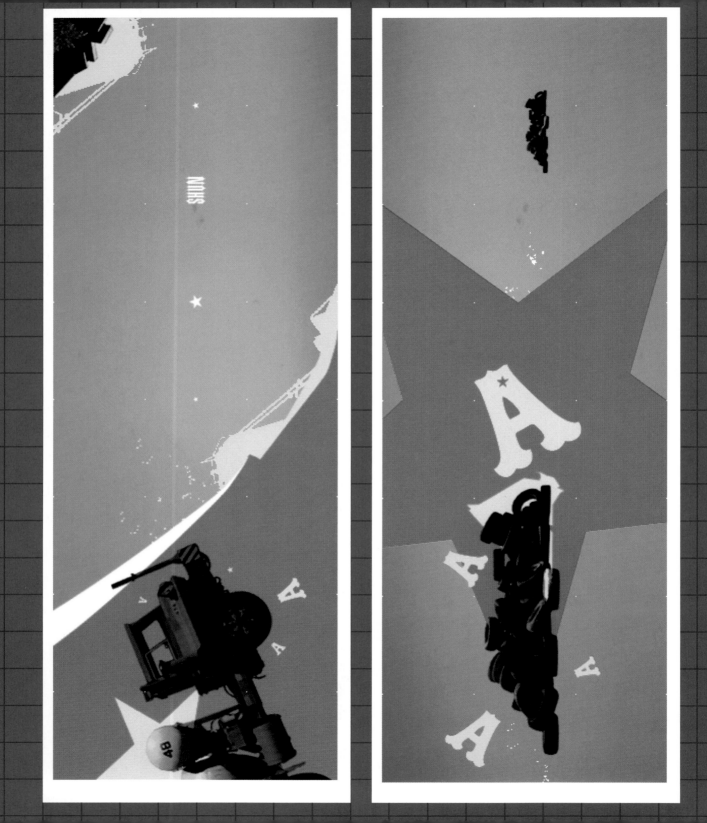

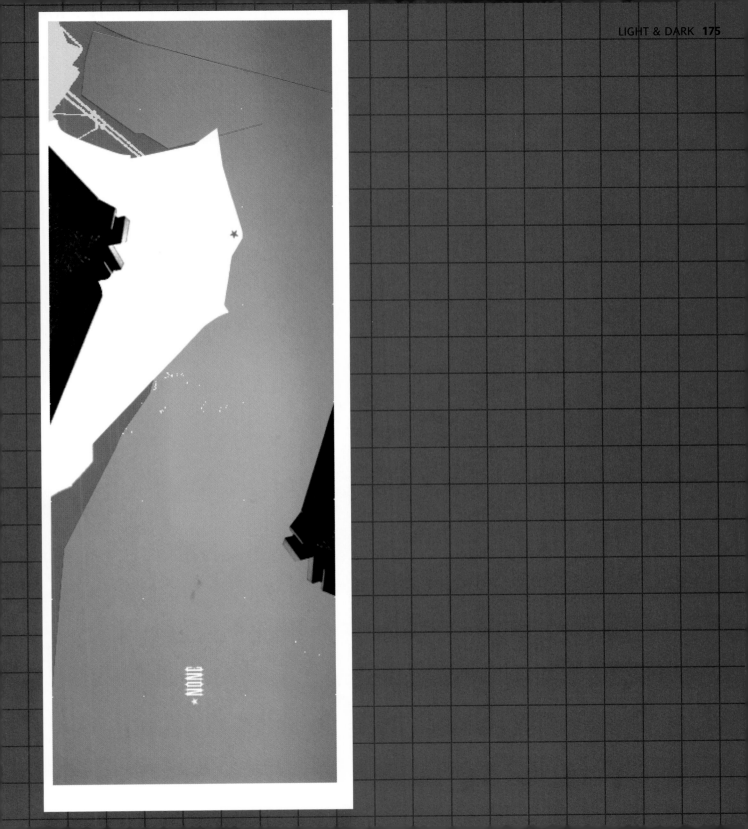

On my site, goingonsix.com, two projects that are pretty good examples of this idea are *Postcards to Home* and *Simple Fascinations*. *Postcards* came out of a couple of different things. I was driving home from the train station one afternoon with my brother. I had my miniDV cam with me and started shooting out of the window with no real purpose. I was twisting the camera around, focusing on the rearview mirror, the trees and power lines going by and the road ahead. A couple of weeks later I was sitting at my machine, looking at that video and flipping around in some of my notebooks when I stumbled on a few old postcards a friend of mine had left at my house. On the front were all these old illustrations of mermaids and women putting make-up on with lines like, "You can see for yourself that I want to make up." Clever right? But what is so special about them is that they've all actually been sent to someone and they all have notes on the back. Most had fairly common pleasantries: "Having a great time" and "I'll see you soon." But the one that got my attention said, "Hope I never see you again." To me this was fascinating. Did this person really mean that how it sounds? Or were they having such a great time, wherever they were, that they never wanted to leave? I have no idea, it's from Ohio in 1946 and I wasn't there. I like the fact that I didn't know. I liked that I could fill in the blanks with my own narrative. Watching the video and reading these postcards got me thinking about all the long road trips I'd taken back and forth to college, knowing I'd be gone for months at a time. So I broke out my notebook and starting jotting down things that came into my head about the road and travel, coming and going, leaving things behind and moving on. And with that, it all kind of came together and *Postcards to Home* was born.

It was a similar process with *Simple Fascinations*. I'd lived in my neighborhood for a while and I'd always noticed the abundance of sidewalk kiddie rides. Fire trucks, boats, rocket ships and assorted animals. These things are everywhere. In front of butcher shops, delis, coffee shops, bakeries, the dollar store. There must be thirty of them within a two-block radius! So I took my camera and my DV out for a walk, took photos of the rides and video of the kids playing on them. And as I always do, I broke out the notebook and went to work. As I was writing down some ideas I remembered this burger joint my parents used to take me and my brothers to when we were kids. They had all these little rides too. We used to play on them but what I also remembered was as 'big brother', I'd let my younger brothers ride the rides while I watched and made sure they didn't fall off and get hurt. That's where it all came together for me; now I had something personal to put into it. It wasn't just pictures and video of these rides anymore, it was a story about my brothers and me, and it was something I could put my heart into. Sentimental fool that I am!

"GO FASTER. SLOWER. FASTER. FASTER. THEY'RE GAINING"

SIMPLE

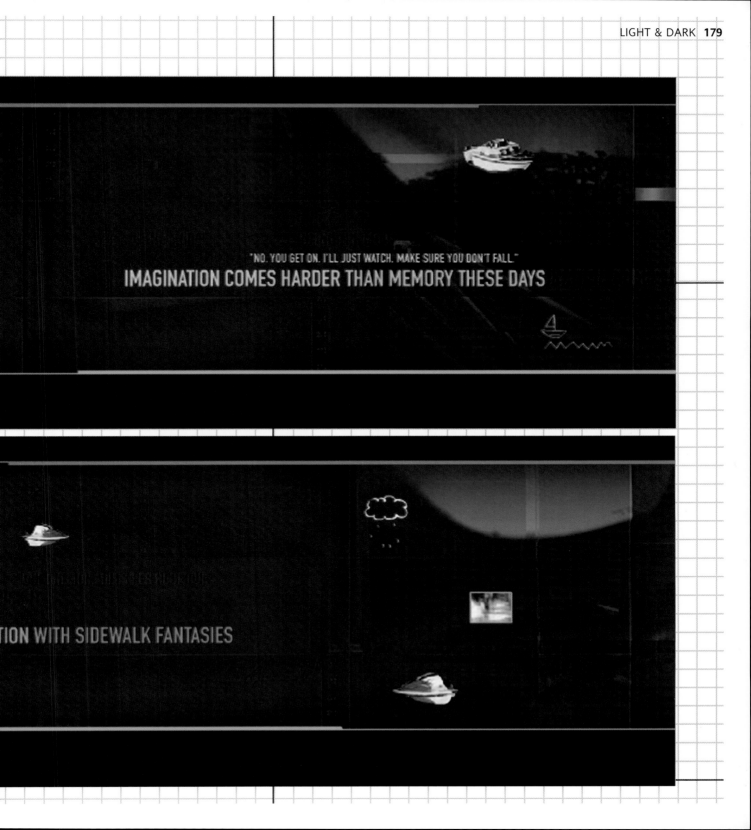

"NO. YOU GET ON. I'LL JUST WATCH. MAKE SURE YOU DON'T FALL."

IMAGINATION COMES HARDER THAN MEMORY THESE DAYS

TION WITH SIDEWALK FANTASIES

So – *Light & Dark*. My first thought was, "What a vague theme". I had no idea what to do or what to think and immediately began over-complicating it in my head. After some thought and ritualistic procrastination I decided to simplify. Light = Good? Dark = Bad? Light: dark: opposite. Then I just kind of took that and thought self-portrait. We've all got our split personalities, our own light and dark so to speak. Anyone who knows me personally knows I don't fall short on that count. Ups, downs, highs, lows, I go through them all. So how would I approach a self-portrait type of piece? I knew I wanted it to be gritty and dirty and bright and clean all at the same time to create this necessary contrast. So what to do?

I've been taking a lot of Polaroids lately, getting some really nice gritty textures shooting directly into refrigerator lights, desk lamps, my living room halogen lamp and things like that. So one really sunny afternoon I stood at my window and took a bunch of photos of my face. The one I finally chose as the main photo seemed appropriate for a couple of reasons. For one thing, I thought the absence of eyes created a nice metaphor about the absence of sight equating to darkness. Secondly, it had some nice color in it that could be pumped up and some good grit. Then I remembered this photo I'd taken recently waiting for the subway. The words *air, live, caution* were spray-painted on the platform. Obviously a warning for MTA workers not to bust into the concrete in that area or something would blow. The way I read it when I took the photo though was almost like a warning about living. I created this little story out of it. Breathe the air, but live life with caution. It made a nice connection and yet another metaphor on the theme. I've recently been introduced to Bruce Mau's *Incomplete Manifesto for Growth* and number 19 states: "Work the metaphor. Every object has the capacity to stand for something other than what is apparent. Work on what it stands for." Well, I'm definitely working it here, and I'm having fun doing it.

I had an idea now and I had some imagery but it didn't feel right without some text. Words of some kind seemed appropriate for some reason. I thought they could add to the piece texturally and hopefully take it to another level. When I was sixteen, my friend Matthew Rienhardt sent me two sheets of typed poems he'd written. I thought they were beautiful then, filled with teenage angst, straight from the heart with glimmers of optimism – they're still beautiful to me now. I read through them and one made sense – it worked for me. I wish I had the capacity to sculpt words in such a visual way.

On and on... I take all of these things, push the pixels around and find a composition that splits the space, the *Light & Dark* so to speak. As for some of the other elements, the star has been a symbol I've used a lot lately. I like stars. They remind me of being a kid in grammar school, when you did something good in class and the teacher would give you a gold or silver star. More nostalgia perhaps. The "H." comes out of something specific. I was listening to Tool's album *Ænima* when I was working on this. Track 3 is simply titled, "H." It's more about the lyrics than it is about the title though.

So this was pretty much my thinking with the *Light & Dark* theme. Maybe it's kind of twisted and weird but these are the things that go through my head when I'm making stuff. I try and analyze every detail to make sure it's appropriate for what I'm doing. I like to play with words and photos, make connections, whether abstract or literal, and see what I come up with. It's like a puzzle, only I never know the outcome. There's never a box top showing me how it all fits together. You just have to lay out all of your pieces and play around with them. It's a process, (albeit undefined), but it's important, I think. I definitely rely on certain things to inspire me when it comes to working with new projects. In the past it was even harder for me to get started or inspired for something, but over time and with experience things start to fall into place. Whether you're continually relying on photographs or video or illustrations or sketches or anything that appeals to your individual sensibilities really, you'll always have some kind of starting point. Use your intuition. They say your first guess is always your best, so work from there, from what you know, and hopefully it will all fall into place.

22.
The air breathes sweet memories,
As i lie in the ashes and the dust.
a time that was to me once sacred,
has slipped into oblivion,
and is me no more.
Youth grew tired of my aging bones,
and ran away from me for good.
Love fades away as i beg to taste her kiss once again,
to hold her close to me for what should have been forever,
and to enter her world of beauty and bliss for one last
encounter,
but she is me no more.
Circumstance is cruelty is the last thing i remember telling
myself,
as i join the rocks and the soil,
in search of myself.

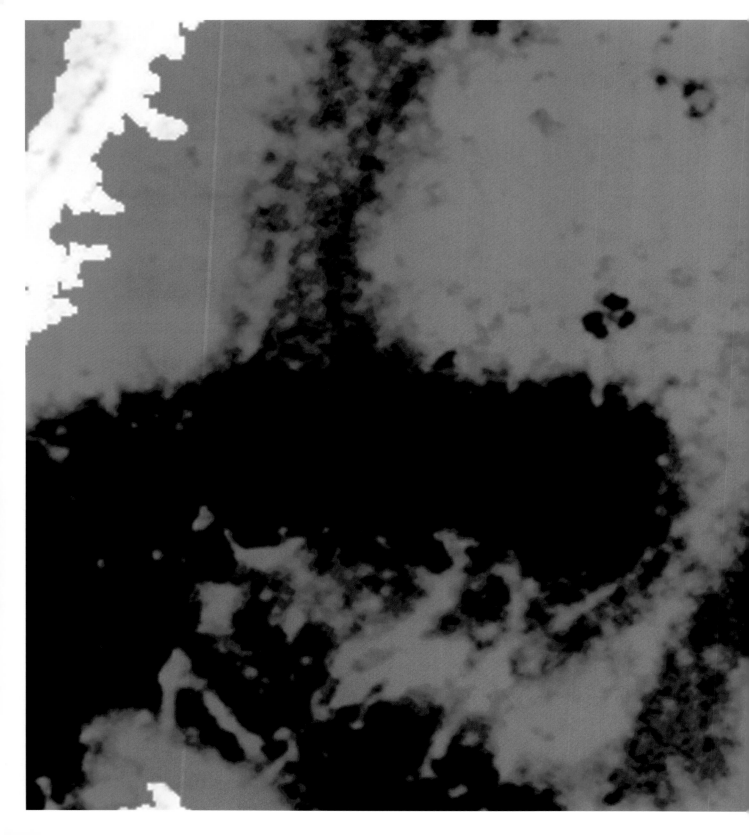

22.
The air breathes sweet memories,
As i lie in the ashes and the dust.
a time that was to be once sacred,
has slipped into oblivion,
and is me no more.
Youth grew tired of my aging bones,
and ran away from me for good.
Love fades away as i beg to taste her kiss once again,
to hold her close to me for what should have been forever,
and to enter her world of beauty and bliss for one last
encounter,
but she is me no more.
Circumstance is cruelly is the last thing i remember telling
myself,
as i join the rocks and the soil,
in search of myself.

e memories,
s and the dust.
e once sacred,
vion,

y aging bones,
for good.
beg to taste her kiss once again,
me for what should have been forever,
d of beauty and bliss for one last

is the last thing i remember telling circumstance is cruelly is the last thi
myself,

d the soil,

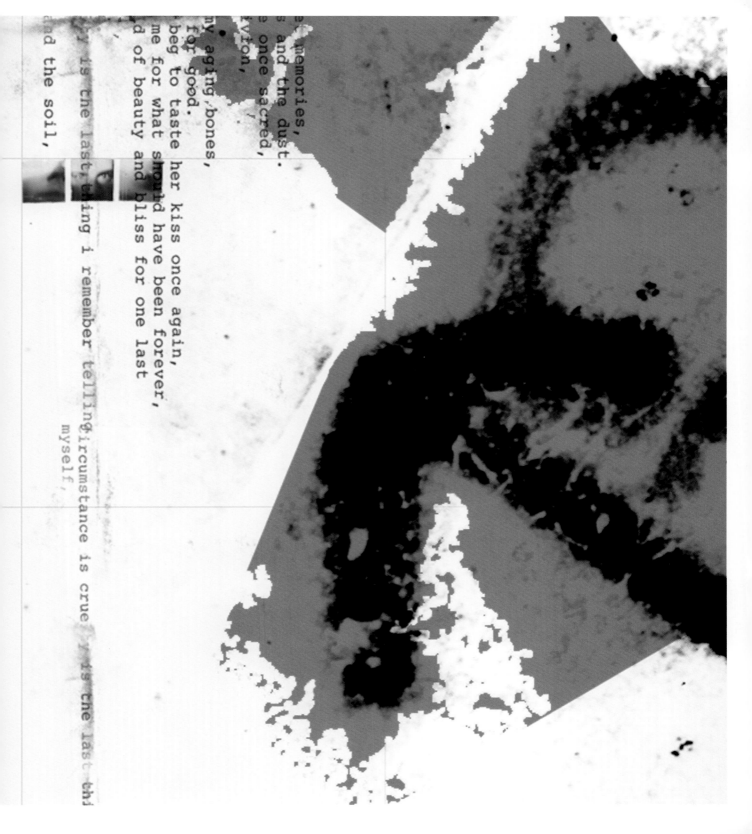

the air breathes sweet memories,
...be in the ashes and the dust.
...time was to be one sacred,
...has slipped into oblivion.
and life no more,
youth grew tired of my aging bones,
...fan away from me, my God.
love fades away as i beg to taste her kiss once again,
to hold her close to me for what should have been forever,
...to after her word of beauty and bliss for one last
encounter,
but there is no more
circumstance is cruel... the last thing i remember telling
myself,
as i join the rocks and the soil,
in search of myself.

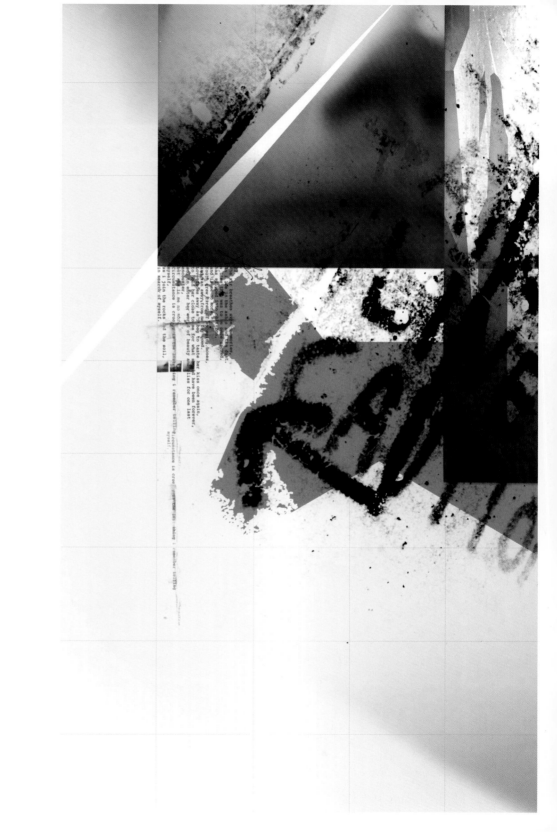

Let's get to grips then with creating some really gritty graphics from photography, using existing photos as image texture. Below I'll take you through my process of composing an image using photography, some simple hand-drawn sketches, and a printed poem.

The specific process I followed will be adhered to, hopefully showing a few useful techniques of composite picture creation. Of course, if you want to produce exactly the same image, then you'll need to use the same components and values that I work with. If, however, you'd like to create something of your own then go ahead and experiment with some of the concepts I introduce.

Whichever path you choose, let's get started with...

Setting up the file

In Photoshop, create a new document and save it as light_dark.psd. Measuring in inches it should be 8.125 x 9, with a resolution of 300dpi, and a white background. With the rulers on display, pull out guides and place them at every inch marker to create an 8 x 9 grid. I find this preferable to the easier, though more constrictive, method of view > show grid (cmd+" / ctrl+"). But of course, work to your own preferences.

I find setting up a grid in my files helps with alignment and acts as a compositional guide should I get stuck balancing the page as a whole.

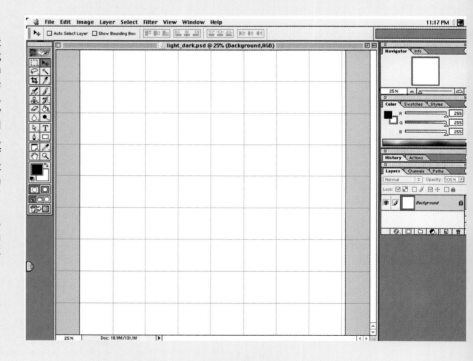

Creating the background

Open the source file called bg_blur.psd. I have no idea what this image actually is but I like it, so I'll use it. It came back with a bunch of photos I took at a New York Yankees game about two years ago. We're going to use this image as a starting point and turn it into a nice soft background for our composition.

What we're interested in with this image is not the color but its tonal range. With this in mind let's try converting the image to Grayscale (Image > Mode > Grayscale), and toning these levels down a bit.

To do this we'll have to adjust the levels (cmd L / ctrl L) and reset the Input Levels to affect the mid-tones of the image. The values I used were 0 / 1.65 / 255.

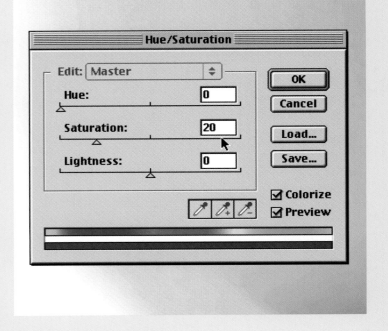

We want to give the image a bit of color so we'll need to convert it back to RGB via Image > Mode > RGB. Then I think we ought to adjust the Hue and Saturation, simply to allow us a greater degree of control over the representation of color within this image.

Beginning with the hue (cmd U / ctrl U) check Colorize, and enter values for each of the three settings. I initially set Hue to 0, Saturation to 20, and Lightness to 0.

The image now has a nice soft red hue to it, but I'm going to adjust the Levels (cmd L / ctrl L) once again to soften the midtones, this time using Input Levels of 0 / 1.40 / 255. Once again your own slant of artistic perception will affect which values you choose here.

Now we have a nice starting point and background for our piece and, if we feel that it needs altering in any way, we can always go back into this layer and tinker with the Levels, and with the Hue and Saturation settings when we put it in to our main document. So let's go ahead and Copy and Paste this image into our main document, light_dark.psd and name the layer bg blur.

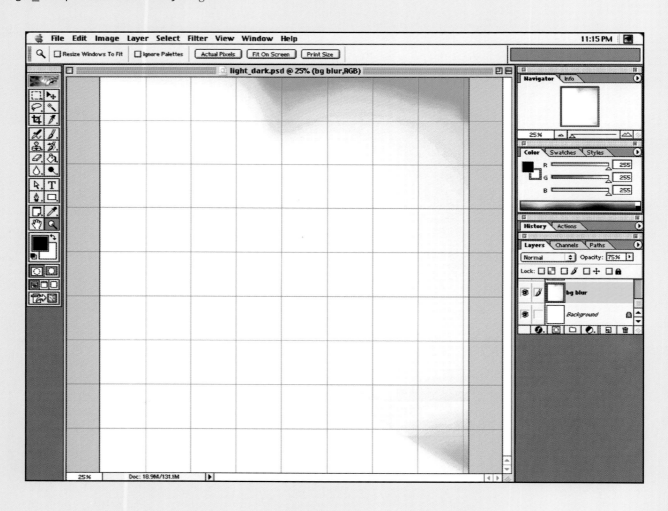

The face

Now we're going to bring in the main image for the piece. Open the file self_polaroids.psd. These are some Polaroids I took of myself when thinking about the theme light and dark. What intrigued me most about the left hand image of the three was the absence of eyes and that there was this sort of bright white glow in their place. This struck me as an interesting metaphor for our *Light & Dark* theme.

With the Square Marquee tool selected, go to the Marquee Options toolbar and in the Style drop down select Fixed Size. When requested we'll need to enter a precise width and height setting, in pixels. Again you can come up with your own values via a trial and error process or, if you're eager to start getting to the more creative aspects, you can copy those that I used: A width value of 1499 pixels and a height of 1553 pixels.

Click anywhere on the image to view the fixed selection and place it just inside the Polaroid's border in the left-most photo.

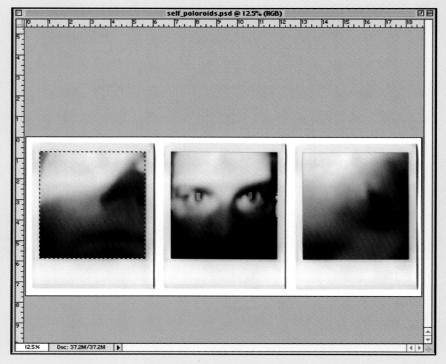

Now Copy and Paste this into light_dark.psd and name the layer main face. Then duplicate this layer via Layer > Duplicate Layer and name the duplicate main face mid. Ensuring this new layer is still current perform an Edit > Transform > Scale (cmd t / ctrl t) and set the Scale Height and Width to 60, in the palette at the top, making sure the link button between them is down to Maintain Aspect Ratio.

In the Layers palette set the Layer Modes for both main face and main face mid to Multiply.

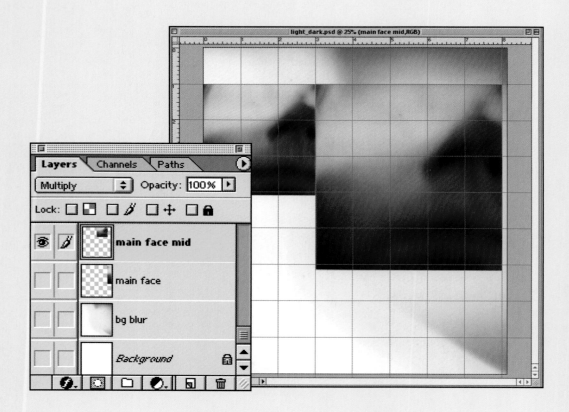

Setting the Layer Modes to Multiply will subtly mix the face images with the background layer bringing through some of its soft tones. For anyone interested in the mechanics of it, Photoshop achieves this result by multiplying the base color by the blend color.

With the Move tool we'll move the main face and main face mid layers into position. This is where the grid we created at the beginning comes into play. You can tweak the positioning pixel by pixel as much as you like and you can play with your own preferences on the overlapping of the images.

At this point we're going to put a white border around the entire page, a favorite technique of mine that I find helps with cropping and positioning. The border kind of crops the whole page nice and neatly, and helps me visualize how the piece will look on an actual printed page.

To achieve this, create a new layer and name it border. Select All (cmd A / ctrl A) and then choose: Edit > Stroke, setting the stroke width to its max of 16, with the Location set to Inside. With the Magic Wand tool, making sure anti-alias is checked off, click anywhere on the inside of the border and repeat the stroke with its max set to 16, so that now the border is a total of 32 pixels on each side of the piece. Repeat this once again so that the border total is 48.

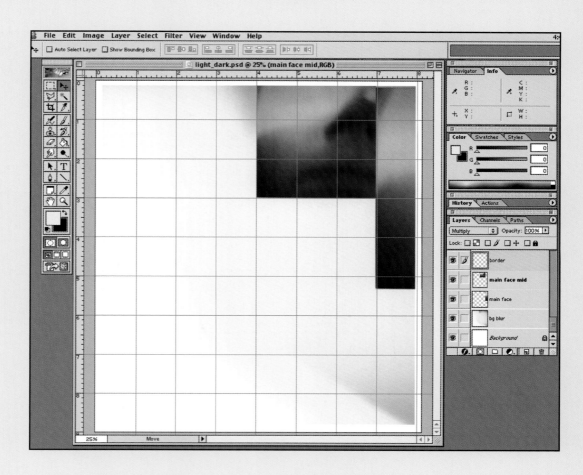

Details 01

Open the source file 6.psd. The numeral is typed in a font called Russell Square. Copy and Paste the 6 layer into light_dark.psd, and name the layer 6.

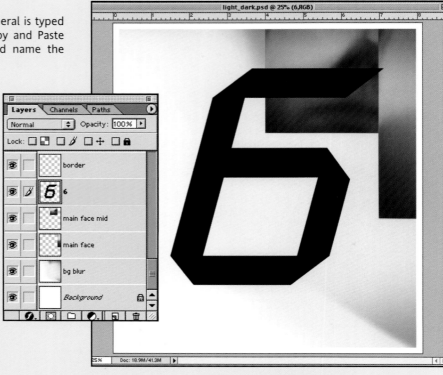

In the Layers palette move 6 so it is positioned underneath the main face mid and main face layers. Next move it to the top right position, shown in the image below, and Invert it (cmd I / ctrl I).

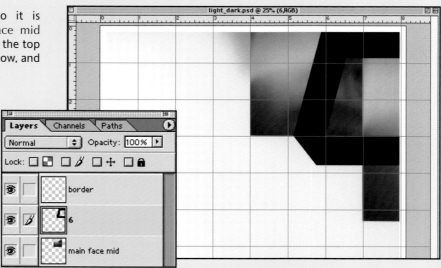

Once the numeral has been inverted you'll notice the nice subtle break it runs through the face images, since their Layer modes are already set to Multiply.

White grad

I really like what the white "6" is doing, as it sits underneath the face images, and to emphasize it I'd like to bring out the white in main face mid layer a bit more by bringing in a gradient and tweaking the layer mode to our favor.

Create a new layer under 6 and call it white grad. With the Square Marquee tool, use the grid of guides to draw a 3x3 square.

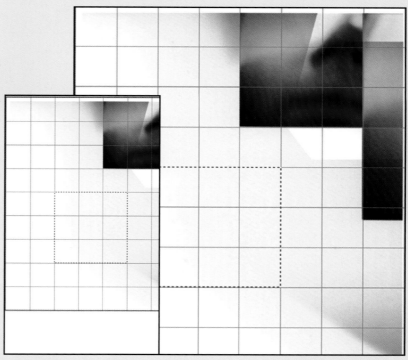

Make sure black is the foreground color in the Toolbar and select the Gradient tool. In the Gradient tool options palette make sure the mode is set to Normal, with the Opacity at 100, the Gradient at Foreground to Transparent, with Transparency and Dither both checked.

With the Gradient tool, hold down the Shift key to constrain it to a 45 degree angle and draw down from the top right corner of our selection to just about the center of the bottom left grid box, as shown in the image right.

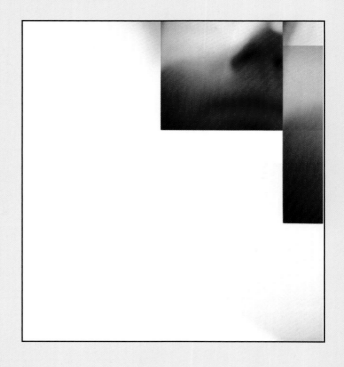

With this achieved, deselect the selection (cmd D / ctrl D).

Now, using the Move tool, move the gradient we just created to the position opposite:

Finally, invert the gradient (cmd I / ctrl I). Simple gradients positioned below or above other images will create some really nice subtle or extreme effects. You may note that the order of layers – where the white grad is in relation to everything else – will change the effect achieved.

Grid

Next we're going to simply trace our grid to make a grid graphic. Create a new layer above the white grad layer and name it grid. In the Colors palette, set R: 154, G: 147, B: 137.

Now select the Line tool. In the Line Options palette click the create filled region button, and set the weight to 1 with the anti-alias box unchecked. With the guides grid turned on, simply draw a straight line for each guide we have set up. Make sure you hold down the Shift key while drawing to ensure a clean line.

In the Layers palette, set the grid layer's opacity to 25 to blend it into the existing image.

Big dirt

In this next step we're going to make some big bad dirt out of a photo taken in the big bad dirty subway system of New York City. We're also going to use this dirt texture with some of the other images we'll import later.

Open the file air_live_caution.psd and convert the image to Grayscale through Image > Mode > Grayscale. Now we need to go into the Levels and blow out the black and white to give the image a super high contrast. Through Image > Adjust > Levels (cmd L / ctrl L) set the Input Levels as follows: 100/0.40/175.

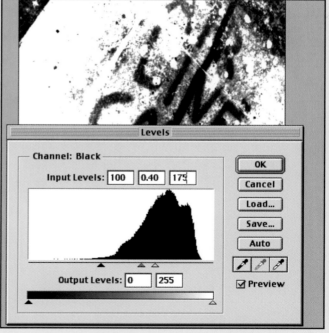

Now we've done that let's go ahead and Copy and Paste this image into light_dark.psd. Name the layer air live caution and make sure it's ordered above everything except the border layer. Fix air live caution to the top right of the image, situated over the top of what we've already done, as shown in the image opposite.

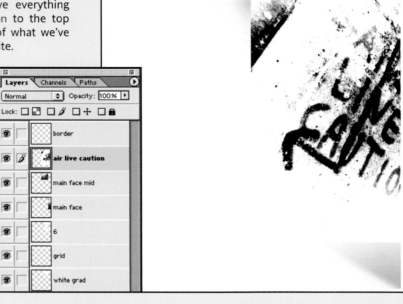

In the Layers palette, set the Layer Mode of air live caution to Multiply.

As you can see, using Multiply will effectively drop out the white from the relevant layer and show the rest of the layers through it.

Big red star

OK, time to fire up Illustrator and open the file star.eps which can be found at www.friendsofed.com/4x4/illustrator/source. Draw a small circle on any side of the star. Duplicate this circle three times and place one on each side of the star as illustrated opposite.

These circles were added because sometimes Photoshop cuts off a couple of pixels from the top and side of shapes pasted in from Illustrator, so, rather than losing any of the star itself, we'll surround it with circles that we don't mind being slashed. Select the star and all the circles (cmd A / ctrl A) and Copy and Paste them into Photoshop. When prompted, make sure Paste as Pixels is selected and Anti-alias is checked and click OK. Name the layer star, move it under the Layer called 6 and erase/delete our four little guardian circles.

In the Tool palette, set the foreground color values to: R: 245, G: 43, B: 42. In the Layer palette, make sure Preserve Transparency (or Lock Transparent Pixels) is checked for our star layer and fill it with the foreground red color (option backspace/alt backspace). With the Move tool, move star to a position where it coincides with all of the other images, as shown in the image opposite.

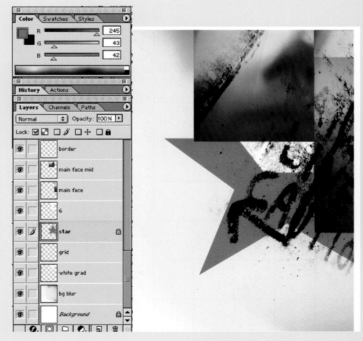

Now we're going to get a little tricky. Select the Magic Wand tool and, in its tool options palette, make sure Tolerance is set to 1 and that both Anti-alias and Contiguous are checked. Contiguous simply ensures that areas selected by the wand are connected to the area clicked – otherwise it will select the entire color range.

In the Layers palette, select the layer called air live caution. Set its Layer Mode to Normal and with the Magic Wand tool click on the large white area in its bottom left. You should end up with a selection that looks something like this:

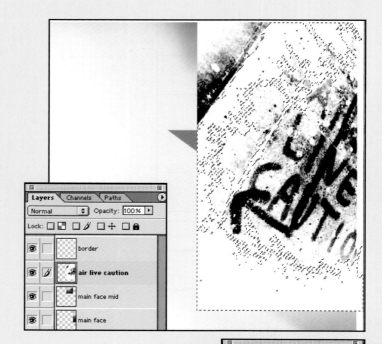

In the Layers palette, set the Layer Mode of air live caution back to Multiply and make the star layer current. With the Magic Wand tool still active, you can move this selection around on the star layer wherever you'd like. We're going to use this rough selection to delete portions of the star so move the selection around as much as you like, deleting as much as you like. I deleted from the star three times and ended up with something that looks like this:

If you're wary of deleting from the layer, make a couple of copies of it and play around till you've got something you're happy with. Don't settle for the first try if you're not happy with it. Undo is your friend and the History Palette is even nicer if you feel you've gone too far.

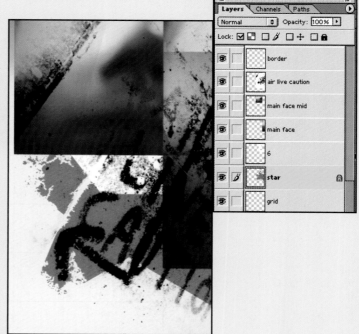

Auto-Illustrator

For our next detail and vector shape I used an application called Auto-Illustrator. It's a crazy generative vector application created by Adrian Ward of Signwave and I like to think of it as Illustrator gone punk rock. A freeware version of Auto-Illustrator can be downloaded at http://www.auto-illustrator.com. It's tons of fun to play with and – heck – it's free! New releases come out pretty often and right now I'm using version beta 0.3-r18 for the Mac.

If you can't get your hands on a copy of Auto-Illustrator I've included the shape created with the tutorial as shape_01.eps, which you can get from www.friendsofed.com/4x4/illustrator/source.

For those of you that have successfully obtained the program, I'll quickly go through how it created this shape. Launch Auto-Illustrator and create a new document. From the Filter menu plough through Filter > Generate > Architecture. Right away the application generates a bunch of beautiful shapes.

Click and drag around in the preview area to move the shapes around in 3D space. Clicking the Empty Space button will obviously empty the space and clicking Add Shapes will, well, add shapes. It's really as simple as that. Play around with it, have fun, and when you've got something you like and that you think might work well with what you're doing click OK. From the File Menu, choose Export > EPS and save your shape. The EPS file created in Auto-Illustrator will open right up in Illustrator for further editing. Add safety circles, as before to prevent cropping when you bring it into Photoshop.

As those of you who know the first thing about random behavior will appreciate, there's very little chance of Auto Illustrator generating precisely the same image for you as it did for me, so for the sake of consistency I'll continue using shape_01.eps for this tutorial.

Copy and Paste shape_01.eps into Photoshop, delete the circles and name the layer vector. Make sure the layer is below air live caution and above all the others. Move vector into position, Invert it (cmd I / ctrl I) and finally, in the Layers palette, set the Layer Mode for vector to Overlay.

I think that this image mixes well with the others in Overlay mode and, more importantly, it acts as a visual device that will direct the viewer's eye to the bottom left of the page. We'll get down there in a little while.

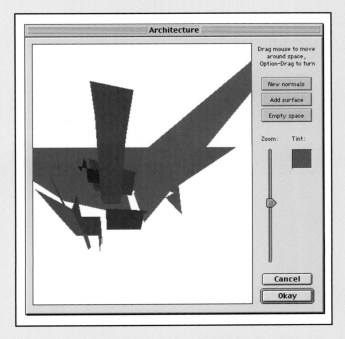

Background again

We're going to add one more very subtle layer to the background of our image. Open the file called subway_door.psd and Copy and Paste this image into light_dark.psd. Name the layer subway door and make sure it's above the star layer.

In the Layers palette, set the Layer Mode of subway door to Overlay and set its Opacity to 50.

It's very subtle but I like what it's doing to the background. The only thing I'm not too crazy about is how it's affecting the star layer.

To improve this, make the layer star the active layer. With the Magic Wand tool (W), click in the largest area of the star. Choose Select > Similar so that the entire star is selected. With the selection still active, make subway door the active layer. Now, delete this selection from subway door.

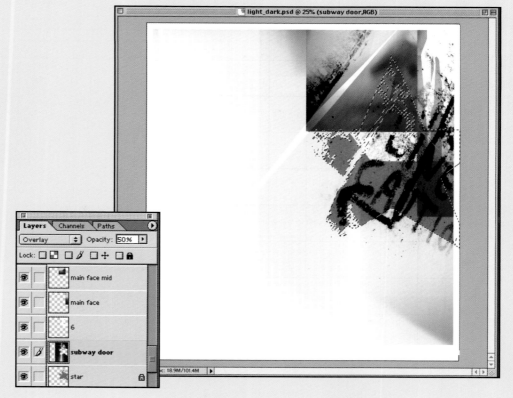

Paper & Poem

Next we're going to incorporate a poem into our piece. It's a scan from the original document that was typed and printed out on a word processor. It's been folded up in a notebook of mine for at least ten years. I think this will fit right into the piece stylistically and the text itself is a big part of the story I'm trying to tell.

Open the file 22_txt.psd. In the same way we treated air live caution we're going to go into the Levels of this image for a higher contrast. First convert the image to Grayscale through Image > Mode > Grayscale. Open the Levels palette (cmd L / ctrl L) and set the Input Levels to reflect your desired appearance. Personally, I used values of: 0 / 1.20 / 245

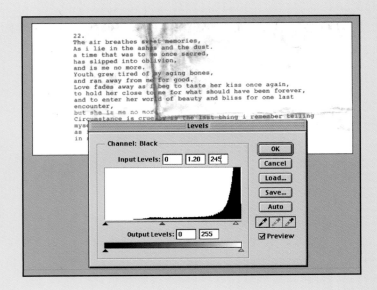

Copy and Paste the image into light_dark.psd, make sure it's above air live caution and name the layer txt paragraph. Set the Layer Mode to Multiply.

You'll notice that there is a defined edge at the top and bottom where the text was cropped. We want to soften that hard edge out so it blends more softly. Select the Eraser tool and in the Options palette set the Erasing Mode to Airbrush and the Pressure to 50. In the Brushes palette, select the standard '100 radius' brush and zoom in to the edge of the text.

Go over the edges with the Airbrush Eraser using lots of short mouse clicks/strokes instead of long ones that produce more of a drawing motion. This technique is more appropriate in this situation based on the imagery, as we're looking for the little inconsistencies that short strokes and clicks will produce. The end result should be something similar to this:

I find that this effect is suitable, but the text of the poem itself appears a little plain and obvious, so let's scale and rotate it. Go through Edit > Transform > Scale (cmd T / ctrl T) and set the Scale Height and Width to 30, making sure you click Maintain Aspect Ratio, and set Rotate to 90. You should end up with something similar to this.

In the Layers palette, set the Opacity for txt paragraph to 90 and move it to the position shown.

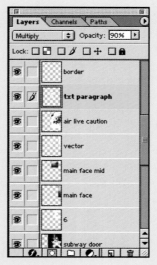

Now, I think this is all working out rather nicely, but I'd like the text to extend further down the page and make a second copy of my favorite line in the poem to reinforce its sentiment a bit. Select the Lasso tool and adjust the Options values so that Feather is 0, with Anti-alias checked. Draw a selection around the line "Circumstance is cruelty is the last thing I remember telling myself". Pick another line if you like, or choose one from your own poem.

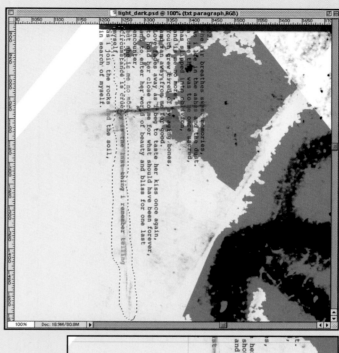

Copy and Paste the selection into its own new layer and call it txt line. Set the Layer Mode to Multiply and move it to a new position:

I think the placement chosen above works as a visual device to carry the viewer's eye from top to bottom, as well as reinforcing the line of text itself. The image is really starting to appear more and more as a coherent whole, as the individual source images become increasingly anonymous.

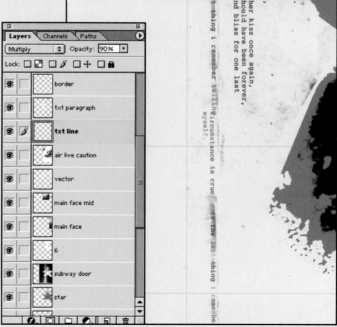

Details 02

OK – lets add another couple of bits and pieces to our creation. First, I feel the upper right of the piece is a bit too white and pure so we're going to create a little bit of dirt to break it up.

Open the file wall_scrapes.psd. Yes – it's as bad as it sounds – we're looking at a portion of the wall in my bathroom. Like we've done in the past, we're going to convert this image to grayscale and go into its Levels so go through: Image > Mode > Grayscale. Open the Levels palette (cmd L / ctrl L) and set the Input Levels as follows: 0 / 0.75 / 175.

Copy and Paste the image into Photoshop, and name the layer dirt top right. Then, Edit > Transform > Flip Vertical before performing an Edit > Transform > Scale, setting the height and width scales to 65, with the Maintain Aspect Ratio button down.

Finally, move the layer into the upper right corner of the page and set its Layer Mode to Multiply.

More faces

Next, re-open the file self_polaroids.psd.

With a Fixed Size Square Marquee of 1499 x 1553, copy and paste each face into light_dark.psd, with each face on its own layer, then link them together.

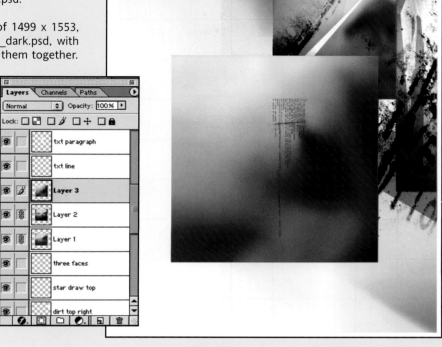

Perform another Edit > Transform > Scale and set Scale Height and Width to 2.5, with the Maintain Aspect Ratio button down. Unlink the three layers and separate each image from the other by 5 or 6 pixels.

Next we want to rotate each one a little manually, using the Transform tool (cmd T / ctrl T).

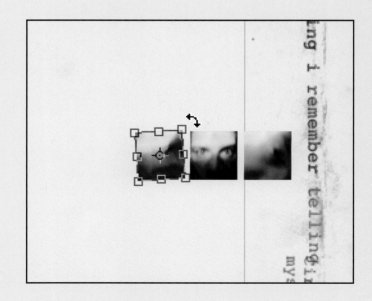

Rotate each one a bit, move them apart by a couple of pixels horizontally and vertically until you're happy. Link the three layers again and merge them (cmd E / ctrl E). Name the Layer three faces and set the Layer Mode to Multiply and the Opacity to 80. Finally, move them into their final position

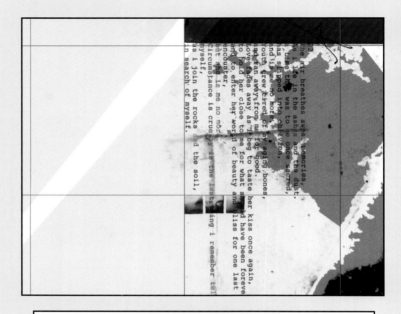

Your file should be looking pretty similar to this:

Hand-drawn text and sketches

I wanted to incorporate hand-drawn elements into this composition to really nail down that personal feel. Simple doodles and drawings can really get that across.

The process is really pretty simple:

Sketch
Scan
Grayscale
Multiply

If you scan a sketch that's not a high enough contrast just jump into Levels and play with the settings. You should have a good idea of how they operate by now.

H.

Start with the file ah.psd – just some letters from a notebook page scanned at 300dpi. Convert the image to Grayscale and Copy and Paste it into light_dark.psd. Name the layer H. Perform another Edit > Transform > Scale and set Height and Width to 50. Set the Layer Mode to Multiply and move it into position.

And that's that.

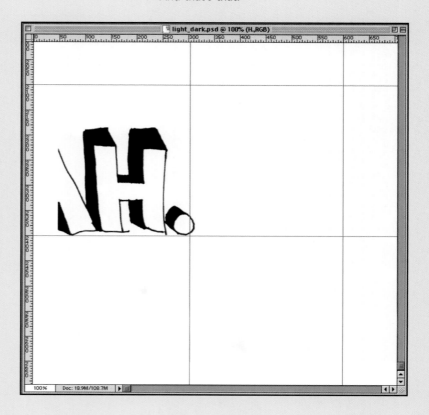

Star

Now open the file sketch.psd. Convert it to Grayscale, open the Levels palette (cmd L / ctrl L) and set the Input Levels as follows: 0 / 0.40 / 230. Now all we want out of this file is that center star. With the Lasso tool, draw a selection around it then Copy and Paste it into Photoshop. Name the layer drawn star bot and put it below layer star and above grid. Flip the Layer on its horizontal and scale it proportionately 50%. Set the Layer Mode to Multiply and move it into position.

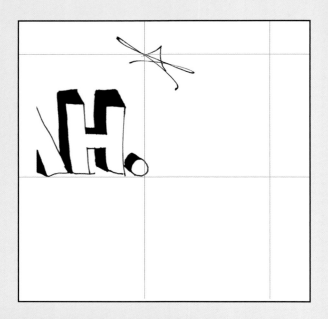

Duplicate the drawn star bot layer, rename it star draw top, scale it down 75%, move the layer above dirt top right, below three faces and move it into position.

Just a couple more steps and details and we'll be done.

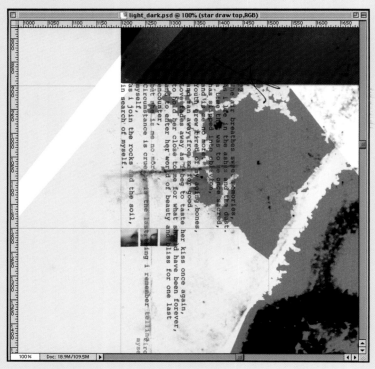

Details 03

In the Layer Palette select the layer air live caution and duplicate it. Move this layer under star and name it dirt bot left. Using the Lasso tool draw out a selection in the left area, similar to the following screenshot.

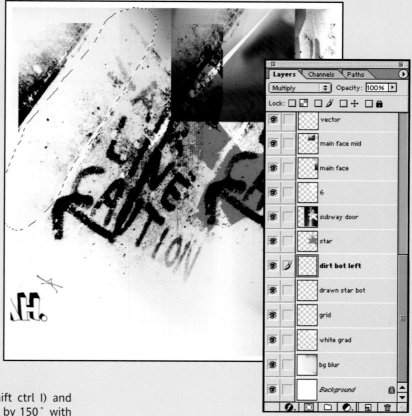

Now invert the selection (shift cmd I / shift ctrl I) and delete the unwanted area. Rotate the layer by 150° with Edit > Transform > Scale , and set the blend mode to Multipy.

Move the layer to the bottom left of the page, to a point that's comfortable for you. I'm only using a portion as an accent to the H and the star, and to create a balance with the dirt going on in the upper right.

Bottom left red

Similar to the dirt, we'll use something we've already created for the red in the lower left. Duplicate the layer star, rename it red bot and move the layer under dirt bot left in the Layers palette. Personally, I chose to use small portions of two red bot layers and this is the result:

Finally, with our guide grid and a selection of 5x9 grid boxes, I created a layer mask on vector, grid and bg blur so that the white background of our image would come through. Here's how our final composition should look:

I've managed to create this image without the use of any filters or fancy plug-ins, just some basic functions in Photoshop and a bit of creativity. Layer modes are a powerful tool so play around with them, experiment. Using simple shapes, gradients and photos you can create some really beautiful effects. You don't have to be a Photoshop guru or Illustrator diehard – just use what you feel comfortable with and use it right!

each author was invited to remix the other works submitted for the book - the following pages display the resulting hybrids

interference is a q and a session with the four authors

noise is the sound of the private discussion forum in which the authors discussed the project with each other

WHAT WAS YOUR INITIAL RESPONSE TO THE OTHER 3 ARTISTS' WORK?

Jemma - I'm familiar with both Sean and Adrian's work — it was great seeing more. It looks like I'm the only one who really used a lot of Illustrator, but this may not be the case, as I haven't seen the tutorials yet.

Sean - I saw Jemma's first. I don't think I was supposed to see it but hey, we're friends, couldn't resist. I wasn't disappointed, it has all that Lentil loveliness I've come to expect over the last year or so. I heard people in Germany like her stuff. I think it's the palette.

I don't know Nick and am not familiar with his work previous to these screens. Pretty interesting. The color has this nice storybook quality to it. I'm especially fond of *Liberty*. It's an image that could have easily come out of Pink Floyd's 'The Wall'. Peculiar and efficient.

I think Adrian's are great. I don't really know Adrian either but I'm familiar with the work he does on Purusdesign. What I most admire about Adrian's work, on the whole, is his sense of color and these pieces are definitely representative of that.

Nick - I had been worried that I might have been doing it "wrong", but I think when I saw the other work, I felt that mine would fit in with the others. I was surprised that we all seemed to use the program in a fairly similar way. Why was I surprised? Perhaps I thought that Photoshop is a bigger thing than it actually is.

Adrian - I was curious. I wondered how four totally segregated artists would approach the theme of *Light & Dark*. When the CD with the high-resolution images arrived, it was much like receiving a birthday gift. I ripped open the packaging and went straight for the files! It was a pleasure viewing the work done by the artists. We all interpreted the theme very differently.

I definitely got a glimpse into how each of the designers thought and saw much deeper than their working canvas.

Jemma's piece is full-on Illustrator. I'd like to get in there and mix things up a bit. I feel the grid coming into play here.

Nick went to town! Pulling out three images reflects his eagerness to give a strong showing. The *Light* piece places me in that environment. I feel the strongest element of this piece is its ability to draw you into the situation occurring within the canvas. There's plenty of emotion coming through here. *Wash* is very cool. I love seeing complexity in work. It seems as if there is only one ground, but in actuality there is a total of three, thanks to the images. Overall the canvas is dark; I wonder what it would look like in a silver monotone print. Hmm.... *Liberty* brings on a modern feeling. There may be an underlying theme, I'd like to find it and amplify it if possible.

Sean's work will be fun to get into. It's rough and dirty. I might have to whip out the scanner and do some classic photocopy wrinkles and scans. I love shifting to a canvas that is out of my range. Usually I create soft and ambiguous imagery. I'm going to have to take my gloves off on this one. Nasty! Awesome Sean!

NICK

HAS YOUR OPINION CHANGED OVER TIME? CONSIDERING EACH WORK IN TURN, WHAT ARE YOUR FAVORITE AND LEAST FAVORITE ASPECTS?

Jemma – Adrian's first piece: I really love the photo layering that I've come to expect from everything at Purus. I remember the first time I really took a lot of notice is when he did that piece for his baby. It was one of the most beautiful things I had ever seen. There's a lot going on in this piece, if you take the time to look. The electric meter is echoed within the piece with the type that appears subtly throughout. The only thing I didn't particularly care for was the drop-shadow on the word 'energy'.

Adrian's second piece: Whoah the colors! Just really beautiful...like a sunset being cast on that beautiful South Californian architecture. I like the type sort of floating or hovering over certain spots. I wish there were glasses you could put on that would float words in your environment for real.

Sean's piece: even when he's being dirty, Sean still maintains the notion of being clean. I've worked side by side with Sean for a long time, and have seen a great deal of his work. No matter what he is doing, there is always good design sense going on with him. This piece carries some great imagery from his hood in Queens. People familiar with NYC will recognize that this is a fairly dirty and visually intense city. In this piece, Sean breaks up that madness with some well thought out white space. I could probably come up with a few narratives in my head surrounding this one, but I know him well... and he has his own story going on.

Nick (*Liberty*): The very first thing that comes to my mind is David Hockney's *A Bigger Splash*. It's those vast flat planes of color. There is something very 80s about this piece, and it becomes a very welcome change of pace in regards to most of the design work I see every day. Then you have this curious opened paper clip. It's the kind of imagery that makes me think of freedom & anarchy – only because paper clips are supposed to remain intact. When someone opens up a paper clip, it is usually out of frustration or something of that sort. Unless, of course, they need to use it to remove a CD from a broken CD-ROM drive...

Nick (*Light*): This is very curious... it looks to me like the station for a train you take to go to Long Island or maybe New Jersey. But there is no signage in view. Again, more flat planes of color, covering what would normally be textured cement and then he adds his own texture. Then the lights above the steps are on. But they normally wouldn't be at the time of day this is set in.

Nick (*Wash*): More of his forced flat color planes on this collage/montage of a truck in the city. It's as if he only wants you to focus on the truck and part of the skyline, and forget the facades of the buildings obstructing your view.

Nick - Looking at the other works, I felt that in Adrian's and Sean's I would question the effectiveness of the type as element of the composition. Are we supposed to read it? What does it mean? I am very literal about things like that. I'm not sure what the type is supposed to say directly, or is it intended to be evocative on a more abstract level? The typographic element in Jemma's is at a different level, it is the sculptural center of the picture. Now, is working on the words "light and dark" actually a piece of work about light and dark? That is a different question. As I have said somewhere else, I am very literal about briefs, whether that is a good or bad thing, someone else can decide.

Sean – I think I'd change mine. I've been looking at it too long. I think maybe I'd go back into the left side and try to resolve it a bit more. I like the starkness of it in contrast to the rest of the piece but something about it irks me a bit. I just can't seem to figure it out though.

In Nick's piece, *Wash*, I'd go in and airbrush out the 'Ford' logo, the 'F150' and the dealership logo. Stuff like that bugs me unless it's an ad for Ford Trucks. Of course the New York license plate doesn't bother me much! Otherwise I really enjoy them all.

Adrian – I haven't given myself the chance to change my train of thought. I glimpsed at the other images for a few minutes when I first received the CD, but I haven't reviewed the images since then. I wanted this to be freestyle on my part. You know, spontaneous and open. Most of the canvases seem to be unfinished. It's as if they're waiting to be completed. I can't wait to jump on them.

I'm a bit challenged by Nick's *Liberty* piece. I know that he is working with the underlying theme of modernism and minimalism. But how do you add to a minimalist piece?

Also in Jemma's piece, I'm curious as to what angle I should come in from. I've been looking at the canvas from different perspectives and doing some "what ifs". This is all very interesting and new to me.

DO YOU THINK THE OTHER ARTISTS HAVE RESPONDED WELL TO THE THEME THEY WERE PRESENTED WITH?

Jemma – Yeah, they've responded well... actually a bit more literally than I have... but I'm always the chump. Each piece has a definite light & dark balance struggle going on.

Sean – I think they've responded well to the theme. The approaches overall are very unique and I think that's great. For me, it's hard to break down their reactions just based on the visual though. It seems to me there would need to be some sort of actual discussion, preferably face-to-face.

Nick – I once made some black mirrors, using sheets of glass painted on the back, I think these were much better at working with dark as a subject. Digital methods are not always the best. They are limited in the way they can affect your senses. If you showed the work to someone and asked, "What is this about?" Would they say, "Oh, light and dark?" I'm not sure that they would, in response to any of our solutions. Sean in particular seems to be working with symbols, as is Jemma. I wanted to try to describe light and dark. I probably had more fun when I stopped worrying about this, but then that is what working to a brief does.

Adrian – I think the artists have responded sufficiently. During this next phase of re-works with each other's canvases is where we'll really see the magic happen. All of the canvases have light and dark surfaces. I'm eager to see what will be done with my pieces.

HOW DO YOU FEEL ABOUT YOUR OWN WORK WHEN SET AGAINST THE OTHERS?

NICK vs ADRIAN

Adrian – Heavily image based and complex. When peering into the working documents of the other designers I saw a bit of them in me. It's different once you actually see into the working documents.

Nick – I think I have tried to hide the fact that I am using Photoshop or Illustrator more. Where I have used a photograph, I have retouched it, however radically, rather than obviously manipulating it in Photoshop. I have not used filters and transparency as much as the other three, I think.

Particularly when I was looking at Adrian's files, I was confused by what was going on with some layers. I realized that it was because he had used those blending modes, like Screen, Multiply, and Dissolve. I have never found these useful, in fact I've always found them very confusing. I found it unhelpful that they produced unexpected effects as I examined the various layers of Adrian's work.

Jemma – Other than the obvious, that my piece has no photography in it, you can see that I rely on Illustrator a bit more than the others. Well, I am thinking Nick uses Illustrator quite a bit, in particular for his first piece with the paper clip.

Sean – It's a nice contrast. Aside from Jemma's there's a great use of photography and I think we've covered quite a nice spectrum in terms of execution. If I stood in a police line-up next to Jemma, Nick and Adrian, the cops would know which one of us was guilty of a piece of work right away, we all have our own style!

REGARDING THE TECHNICAL ASPECTS OF THE OTHER WORKS, WHAT CAN YOU LEARN FROM? IS THERE ANYTHING IN YOUR CONTRIBUTION THAT YOU'D NOW APPROACH DIFFERENTLY?

Sean – I'm not sure about this actually. I was kind of relieved when I looked through the Photoshop files and saw how simply they're constructed. It was cool looking at Adrian's because we use some similar techniques that achieve similar effects. The difference is how we use them though so it's pretty interesting for me.

I like Jemma's idea on breaking plug-ins. She must crash a lot. Actually I know she does! Sometimes I think the plug-ins are going to crash her!

Jemma – There's always stuff to be learned from the process of others. It's nice to see how each person approaches the subject differently... and how a blank canvas is treated differently.

Nick – I was surprised at how easy I found it to look through the other works and understand how they had been put together. Jemma uses filters a lot. Or abuses filters a lot. I like the way that she seems to push them to the point where they produce unlikely and interesting results. It is extracting a more organic way of working from what appears to be a very predictable machine.

Adrian – I'm a bit curious about Jemma's approach to the grid. I've passed over the method a few years back but haven't touched it since. I felt a bit claustrophobic and restrained. But other designers can't work without it. Maybe my perception of the idea has been contaminated by my first experiences. Now would be a good time to dip into to it once again and see what's up.

As I mentioned before, Adrian, and I think Sean, use those blending modes in Photoshop, which confuse me. I have read the descriptions of these modes in the manuals, and I find them completely baffling. I prefer to use effects that have more direct analog equivalents, like blur (which I hardly ever use, actually) opacity and contrast. I think it is simpler to use these functions rather than the blending modes since they make the relationship of individual layers in the file more predictable. I prefer to be as simple as I can.

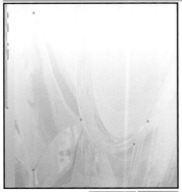

ADRIAN vs JEMMA

LOOKING AT THE STYLES OF THE FOUR ARTISTS HERE, DO YOU THINK THEY FORM A GOOD SNAPSHOT OF WHERE DIGITAL DESIGN IS HEADED TODAY?

Nick – I don't know. I'm sorry, I don't know.

Adrian - Interesting question. I see a youthful voice waiting to be heard. Sean exhibits strength and aggressiveness. Jemma's canvas is structured and ideal. Nicks work is floating and full of charisma.

All of the methods used here are just a sample of what we will see in the future. Even if we worked for 80 hours on 10 separate canvases I feel we would have still only begun to scratch to possibilities of the future.

Also in what medium we see the work in will define its true presence.

Sean – Like I said, I think this is a nice range. I'd like to think we're all just designers who happen to be working in the 'digital' realm.

Jemma – I think there are too many directions we are going in to try and pin it down to a couple techniques or styles. I like diversity. More is better. Why bore the lot of us with the same derivative crap.

WHAT COLLABORATIVE PROJECTS HAVE YOU TRIED IN THE PAST? WHAT ARE YOUR FEELINGS ABOUT THIS, AND OTHER, COLLABORATIONS?

Jemma – I've collaborated quite a bit in the past, and many of the projects I will be involved with in the near future will be work with others.

I've worked with Mike Cina – www.weworkforthem.com – and we regularly pass Illustrator and Photoshop files back and forth. Sometimes we rock out on these things we call 'swamp battles', where files are passed back and forth giving each of us a maximum of five minutes to work on them. It's kind of stressed and rushed, but a good exercise, one that I would recommend to anyone.

I've also done a lot of work with Damian Stephens, creative director for www.type01.com in Cape Town, South Africa. This is less actual design collaboration, but more along the lines of Net-based concept building and brand development for a private project under www.h-corps.com – we offer publicly the one Cycle.Occur project – www.onecycleoccur.com, which is on no set schedule and has featured Tomato Interactive and Ubermorgan in the past.

Something I do regularly is give away Illustrator files. In addition to giving out a set to the general public, I have given series made specifically for certain friends. A couple of directories have been set up for Joshua Davis in the past, and now you can find many of my vectors on www.PrayStation.com and www.once-upon-a-forest.com – including a nifty screensaver Josh put together with my work.

Next up is a very exciting project with Christian Zander - www.zander.dk – from Copenhagen, Denmark. It will revolve around our daily lives and how we move about in our respective environments. I'm looking forward to it.

I think these 'give and take' collaborations are great. Nothing bad can come of them. That whole third-mind thing takes over and both parties stand to learn a lot.

Nick – As an illustrator, usually I am left to be quite independent. Sometimes though I have worked with designers who want to be actively involved. It has usually been a very good experience to collaborate. It does arrive at a sum greater than its parts, usually. Having said that, I normally prefer to work on my own.

It's an easy way out. It's an easy solution. But when nothing else appears, nothing comes to save you, what else can you do?

The psychiatrist that I finally managed to see tells me that with some work and prescribed medication, I can eventually work out my feelings and become a well-adjusted human being.

"You're gonna fix me?" I ask him. "There's nothing wrong with you. Nothing that a little work can't help."

4:37   5:03   5:14   5:26

4:37 PM
TUESDAY, AUGUST 15, 2000

SEAN http://www.bornmagazine.com

Sean – I worked on a piece for Born magazine (http://www.bornmag.com) called *My X-Files*. I was given a 15 year-old girl's journal entries from a single day and my job was to interpret her words. What she wrote is emotionally quite intense and very long. It was tough but I think we did a great job. Most importantly though, she was happy with the outcome and that meant a lot to me.

In college I did a five minute video with a friend of mine. It was a video for a song by Tool. We worked really well together. At first it was tough delegating responsibility but we worked through it. We've been apart for a couple years but are planning something now. Should be interesting since he's in Portland and I'm in New York and we want to do another video. Good thing we've both got broadband hook-ups! To this day I think he's one of the only people I'd have success and fun collaborating with. Finding the right person or people to work with is the key to collaboration because not everyone is going to mesh.

Was this project a collaboration? I didn't work with anyone. I mean, I'll remix the other works but that to me really isn't collaborating, it's trading files.

Adrian – Not many. I'm eager to do so in the future with elite groups willing to work out of the box, and not only for print. I have a few friends interested in doing installation art. I think this is where I'll end up in the long run.

WHY DO YOU DO THIS STUFF? WHO DO YOU THINK YOUR AUDIENCE IS? WILL DESIGN FOR DESIGN'S SAKE BECOME A MORE MAINSTREAM ART FORM?

Sean – It's what I always wanted to do plus I'm not really qualified to do anything else. Maybe manual labor, which isn't so bad. I'd probably be in better shape from not sitting in front of a computer all day.

My audience? Hmmm, I don't really know. My friends like my stuff, and my family likes it. I get email from people all over the world who like it and seem to come back for more and I'm glad they enjoy it.

Adrian – I do this to move people. When I was starting out as a new media artist and designer I was hungry for inspiration. Communication Arts and Critique magazine always came up short. The work in there is so mainstream it makes me nauseous. I'm not interested in creating average solutions for average clients. It's boring to me. I'm interested in changing the world of new media. I know the task is beyond me, but with a handful of elite designers, the task doesn't seem so daunting. My preference is to create vehicles for inspiration. And the more people I can reach, the better.

ADRIAN vs SEAN

NICK vs JEMMA

Nick – Why do I do it? Curiosity and excitement about visual experience, I suppose. When I used to paint, it was a very different set of interests, narrative, historical and political. Working with Photoshop it is a direct manipulation of visual experience. Design for design's sake sounds very undesirable. The boundaries between fine art, illustration and graphic design are in question here. I think that pure graphic design, without a subject to serve, seems very empty, unless it is very decorative. There are some books around with very vague *raisons d'etre*.

Who is my audience? When I am commissioned as an illustrator, this is very easy. I am illustrating or advertising to whoever or whatever my client is concerned with. This is one of the very good things about commercial illustration: you are given an audience, what you do gets seen. I do other work though, which really has no audience at all. This does not make me any less keen on making it. I really just make it for myself. What sort of an audience can you expect for cross-stitch embroidery? I make quite a lot of work that just hangs around the house. I suppose it is up to me to find an audience. I don't think people are actively hostile to cross-stitch embroidery.

Jemma – Because it amuses me. Why else would I do it? Maybe to help mold my surroundings. I like new things to look at. So why wait around for someone else to do what I could do myself?

I think I have a big audience in Germany. I get a lot of mails from Germans. I should just put an end to the copy on Prate being in English. I don't consider art and design the same disciplines. They are similar only via the visual aspects. To think otherwise would be absurd.

WHO WOULD HAVE BEEN YOUR THREE DREAM COLLABORATORS - LIVING OR DEAD? WHY?

Adrian – Arnaud Mercier of http://elixirstudio.com just cause he's such a powerhouse of a designer. The guy can do it all.

Bradley Grosh of http://www.gmunk.com because he's a big pimp and big pimps can rock the canvas.

Hmm... James Widegreen of http://threeoh.com. James has been a mentor to many designers within the Vir2l family. He's such a smart and talented designer. And there's nothing better than smart design.

Jemma – Bill Drummond of www.penkiln-burn.com – I'd really be dreaming if that happened. And no, it most likely wouldn't be design oriented.

Lia of www.turux.org. I would love to design a small-run book featuring screen shots of her work.

Sean – Derek Riggs, Iron Maiden, Eddie. Up the Irons!

Nick – What I have found most useful about using a computer is how it means that you do not have to collaborate with anyone. You do not need other technologies to deliver your work, you do it all on your Mac. So it is not technical reasons that encourage you into collaboration.

I will answer a different question. Three collaborations that I want to see completed:

An opera on the life of Emiliano Zapata. I don't think I have the technical expertise to help here though. Andrew Lloyd Webber?

A massive budget film about Henri Christoph, Toussaint L'Ouverture and the slave revolts in Haiti. Spike Lee as director? I could do a poster.

I would really like to work with something musical. Anything interesting, new, and probably Brazillian.

HAS YOUR WORK CHANGED RADICALLY OVER TIME? HAVE THERE BEEN ANY SIGNIFICANT SHOCKS TO YOUR SYSTEM THAT HAVE CHANGED YOUR WORKING METHODS?

Sean – My 'work' isn't really important right now. It's mostly been a good distraction, hard to concentrate though.

I'm a New Yorker. I love NYC, always have and always will. During this book the World Trade Center went down. It was a pretty big shock to my system as I watched most of it happen right in front of me. I haven't felt like doing much lately except being with family and friends. Maybe in the future I'll get into construction. I wouldn't mind being part of whatever it takes to rebuild the area. We'll see I guess.

Nick – Of course my work has changed a lot over time, but at the same time I'm not sure that I have ever surprised people who have known what I have been doing over the course of my career. I think an illustrator accepts being responsive to the material that s/he is commissioned to work with, which means accepting at least a compromise on the way your work develops. Hopefully, in the background your own progress unfolds.

Adrian – My work has changed a bit. I'm going through a phase of freestyle at the moment. I'm focusing on imagery and type. I know I need to push type more, so I'm looking into the Adobe and émigré font libraries. Also I'm interested in looking into some of Cina's (http://www.trueistrue.com) homemade fonts. I asked him for a copy a while back and he snapped! Hehe. I'll have to pay for 'em like everyone else. Oh Mikey.

Jemma – I can say this; the more I work, the more I learn, the more I have to offer. Simple as that. If anything has accelerated this rate of progress, it would have to be the moment I told myself to stop messing around and get serious.

IS THERE ANY MEDIUM AROUND THAT YOU FIND DOESN'T WORK/DOESN'T CONTAIN THE TENSIONS REQUIRED FOR RELEVANT ARTISTIC EXPRESSION? IS THERE A MEDIUM YOU'VE YET TO EXPLORE, BUT WHICH SEEMS TO HOLD A LOT OF PROMISE?

Jemma – What? No. Hmmm... actually... yeah. Industrial diving. Under-water, deep-sea welding. That's the future. No joke.

Sean – I'm open to all media really. I'd like to work with video more. Short films maybe. I've got an idea for at least one. Maybe build something with my own hands instead of with a mouse for once. That'd be interesting.

Adrian – The Internet is still in its youth. And in such a young phase it's difficult for it to be a medium for inspiration. I'm waiting for gigabyte bandwidth and full on motion graphic interfaces. It's not about 28.8 k and dial up compressions anymore. And that's a relief, that was so depressing.

I'm interested in getting into 3D creation. I have plenty of concepts that I'd like to execute with the aid of Studio Max. My first endeavor with that will be a mechanical insect. Something that projects animation onto the wall of a synthetic arena. There's plenty of room for concept development here.

Nick – What a strange question. Honestly, I have thought that I would like to do some marquetry. I have the very subject ready. (Marquetry is not the same as macramé. Macramé as yet I have not seen as containing...) Any means necessary.

IF YOU HAD THE EXPERTISE AND MONEY TO CREATE THE ULTIMATE IMAGE MANIPULATION/DIGITAL DESIGN SOFTWARE – WHAT WOULD IT DO? WHAT CONSTRAINS YOU IN CURRENT APPLICATIONS?

Sean – Software is cumbersome enough as it is. After Effects kicks my ass, so does 3D studio max. I can barely wrap my head around the stuff I use let alone making any of it bigger or more powerful.

Nick – Really, apart from little pieces of difficulty operating them, I have never felt constrained by any programs. I just don't have the kind of imagination that is ambitious for new programs. I am more worried that digital equivalents are replacing actual experience. I have seen a digital simulator of riding a bike. Why?

Jemma – I'd have Adrian Ward build it, and other than being vector based, I'd trust him completely in concept and production. Ade rocks steady. Word.

Adrian – It would work opposite the Operating System. If the application froze or crashed from intensive calculations it could be restarted without stalling the entire system. The software would work in real-time without the need for waiting when applying serious effects and saving documents. The application would combine 3D, raster imaging, motion graphics and vector layout all in one.

If I had the money, I'd create a refuge for new media designers willing to create media that would make this world a better place. Actually Mike Cina and I were talking about this.

This refuge would be in a discreet location somewhere in the world, and the artists would be selected by invite only. This in turn would elevate the invitation's value. Imagine being one of a million designers getting invited to come and play with the best new media designers in the world! In turn for their dedication I would supply them with room and board and clear any existing debt they may have. They would be supplied with dual 1.8 ghz PC's or dual 800 Macs with triple 22 inch panoramic displays and maxed out with 1.5gb of ram all dedicated to Photoshop. Their workstations would be sub-sea level and just so sweet with modern architecture and design throughout the facility. Something like a concrete bomb bunker comes to mind.

But, not until I get paid I guess. Bids anyone?

DO YOU KNOW WHAT DIRECTION YOU ARE HEADED FOR THE FUTURE?

Sean – I have no idea. Just trying to keep on keepin' on really. I wouldn't mind trying to teach, maybe work with kids in some way.

Adrian – Not really. I don't tend to think beyond the scope of two months much. But when pressed to answer, I hope to pass what I have learned onto young and training designers. I'm instructing part time at the Art Institute of Southern California. I think this will lead into a career as a New Media philosopher of sorts, or a lazy butt that plays games all day!

Nick – I am largely directed by commissioned work. I would like to do some more work on ceramics. I would like to be able to take better photographs. I would like to take some moving pictures.

Jemma – West.

ADRIAN vs SEAN

4x4 **Nick Higgins**
Jemma Gura

FOE

Light & Dark RMX

Illustrator & Photoshop 2001
Friends of Ed

delivery date:
082201

theme:
light&dark

project:
4x4

friends/of/ed

GeSTALT

A physical, **biological**, psychological, or **symbolic** configuration or pattern of elements so unified as a whole that its properties cannot be derived from a simple summation of its p

ADRIAN vs NICK

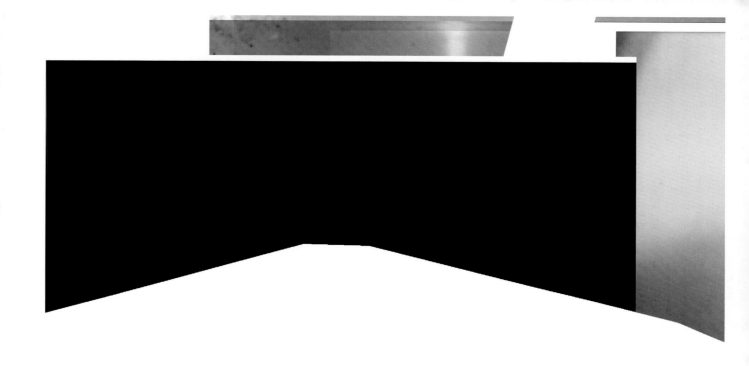

END OF THE BEGINNING

Adrian – From what I have seen from the finished work we all approached the brief of *Light & Dark* very differently. Some chose to take a literal route, and others took a more subliminal route.

All I know is that I can't wait to allocate that RAM to Photoshop and throw in my ten cents to each image on the CD.

Awesome everyone!

BEGINNING OF THE END

Nick – I have just started to open up the remixes, and I'm really excited by them. I will look at them for a bit at leisure and then try to post something wise and uncannily perceptive. Straight away though, I think they look really strong as a set, so far. I couldn't even recognise my stuff in Jemma's picture, even though I liked it a lot. It makes me think I should have been more positive about collaboration in the Interference section.

Adrian – Working with all of the originals was a fun deal. So far what I have seen from Sean and Jemma is blowing me away. They're my images, but treated by someone else. It's like déjà vu. Strange! And very cool.

Now I'm gonna head over to Sean's revisions! I love those!

Jemma – I guess Sean is right about collaboration... this has definitely been more of a great big remix project, which is cool. We could keep passing files around a little more, time permitting.

Sean – So does there need to be more remixing done, or remixing of remixes?

ED – Don't know about more remixing – it's up to you guys. I'm not sure if the idea of one vast cocktail of all of you is something that appeals or disturbs.

Jemma – I can't be mixed up in a cocktail glass with Sean! It'd be like Bombay Sapphire and an old English 40oz.

PIXEL PERFECT?

ED – In the Interference section said that *Light & Dark* might have been better tackled with some mirrors and black paint. What would you guys have done given carte blanche over medium? Would you always opt for the whole pixel thing anyway? Of course Jemma would always opt for poetry as her medium of choice....

Jemma – Bah, I hate poetry. Maybe I would make a cardboard box... and poke holes in it... then hide inside and take photos. Then maybe stitch them into a Quicktime 3D thingy.

Sean – I would have stuck with pixels.

IN THE MIX

ED – Where has that big scary blood red remix come from, Sean? What images have you thrown in there? It looks like the lift doors opening in *The Shining*.

Jemma – I love that red bloody mess... it's like meaty.

Sean – The big red things are a combination of Jemma's 3D shape and my broken up stars. I've been watching too much CNN.

ED – The Sean remix (the white & blue architectural design) is really disorienting.

Jemma – he's the new Zaha Hadid. The sort of architecture that makes you feel you don't know which way is up. Like you said, disorienting. It's like the Guggenhiem here, or the Belgo restaurants. They make me feel sick… vertigo.

ED – How can something abstract seem upside down?

Jemma – M C Escher did that quite well, don't you think?

ED – Those two remixes of Sean's were both a bit scary, in very different ways.

Sean – Made you a little uncomfortable huh? That's a good thing.

ED – One's really bleak and the other one's really hectic and full on. Do you think these have been affected by the World Trade Center horror happening just down the road from you while you were working on these projects?

Sean – What happened in New York has definitely been insane for me. Watching it happen, breaking down two days later, hearing the stories of friends in the building who, thank God, got out. It's inescapable and I refuse to put it by the wayside. My site has been down for 15 days with a link to the Red Cross. When I put it back up there will be links to information on the Red Cross, firefighters, police funds and anything else I can find.

It's hard not to think about if you live here and could once see them from your bedroom window.

I could go on and on…

SEAN vs ADRIAN

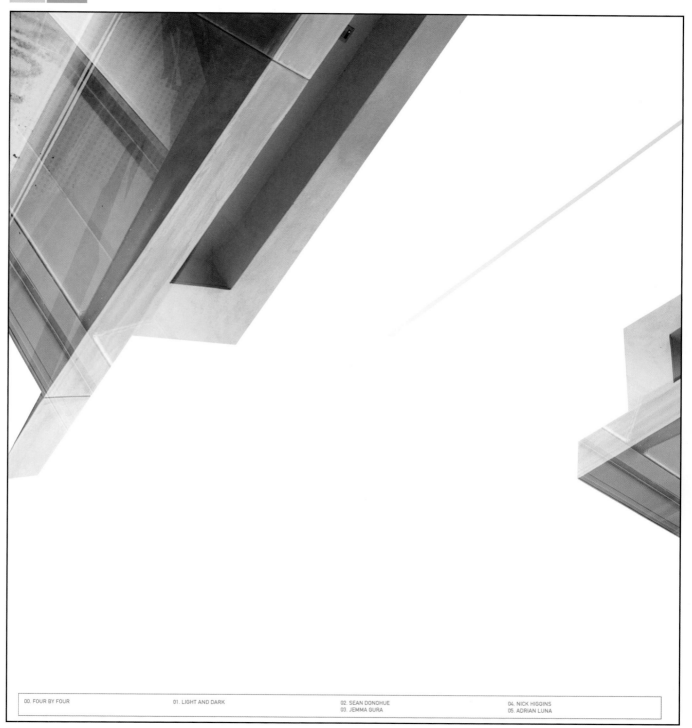

ED – New York has symbolic status for us all.

Sean – Yeah, I think it has actually. We don't really have small buildings or homes as heavily 'designed' in New York City as they must have where Adrian lives. I take a lot of photos of buildings and construction equipment, and I've used them in my work. The newest thing on my site, *The System* shows that. Buildings, cement plants, cement mixers, tires.

I've had an idea for a new site with a new theme for a while and it's kinda leaning in that direction.

Nick – I am curious about the strength of the New York influence too, mainly because I am here in London but two out of three of my pictures were very New York based. This might be because I have a lot of pictures from there, because I did live there for a time.

I thought I was less interested in it visually, mainly because it was so familiar in pictures that it was hard to look at it clearly. Given an open brief though, I ended up back there... Geographically, I did think that what I did to Adrian's picture was to Europeanize it, by making it dark and gray.

Adrian – Funny how the surrounding environment can affect how you visualize. Sometimes you may not even know it, but influence can overwhelm. It's all part of the human psyche of absorption I guess. It makes sense.

In that case, are we bound to our surroundings? If I live in Italy, will my design be purely Italian? Is my outlet to the Internet world just a reflection of that domain?

Gosh. Too much espresso this morning. They shouldn't have these coffee machines available to the public. We abuse them!

NICK vs ADRIAN

ED – Did anyone disagree with what was done to their work? The abandonment of control must be quite an issue.

Adrian – I thought it would be easy to just continue the working process, but it wasn't. It's like working on another artist's dry canvas. Also, it's like being painted into a corner. I felt as if the work given to me was already near completion, so I had to start fresh. My solution was easy. I attempted to retain some of the integrity of the original piece, because I don't want to stomp on the efforts contributed by the original artist. By keeping the integrity, I mean bringing over the same color palette and overall composition. Major changes, with the same overall tone and theme.

Jemma's is a good example. I kept her same hue while adding some of my personal imagery. Instead of continuing on the original canvas, I decided to create a new document in Photoshop and then proceeded to drag and drop certain elements from the original piece. This made everything so simple for me. It gave me control over the elements. I felt as if it was my decision to use what was in that basket, and at the same time, I had my database to grab from while working.

I still want to go back in and do some more work though.

Jemma – Well I have no problems with losing control on my image... a remix is a remix.

ADRIAN vs JEMMA

Nick – I love what Jemma did to my Light picture.
I would like to make things that abstract, but I am
always very literal. I think the remixes really took
off. Is it because we are more relaxed, don't feel
so bothered to come up with something?

JEMMA vs NICK

4x4 **Nick Higgins**
Jemma Gura

FOE

Light & Dark **RMX**

Illustrator & Photoshop **2001**
Friends of Ed

I identified with Adrian's interest in architecture. I think I made his into something European (as I said before). He had Californian light – I made it look like it was raining in Finland – not what I set out to do. Then Sean really emphasized the light in it. I think the very light touch of Adrian's remixes is great, the white fabric one.

I always put too much in. What he did to my Wash picture was good too – he made it more ambiguous.

ADRIAN vs NICK

Adrian – Jemma your remixes rock my world.

For some reason I'm getting jealous wishing I could have seen it the way you did.

It's like I wish I had that perspective. This is great. Where did you get that font Jemma? The one that says "FOE" at a slant on my master_a.psd?

JEMMA vs ADRIAN

Sean – I think the font Jemma's using is called 'Formation'. I think that Mike Cina guy made it. haha

Jemma – Adrian, I love your remixes. What you did to my piece was way beauteous! The 3D shapes in the background lend a nice atmosphere to everything. And a yes to what Sean said on the font. It's a Cina type... he keeps giving them to me... I think he has a crush on me or something. Woooo!

I'm glad you like what I did to your piece, I had a lot of fun working on it. I'm a sucker for machine type, like on the meter.

For the past six months I've had my head around patterns and machine graphics like receipts and bus passes. When I saw the dial on the electric meter, I immediately wanted to see the printed stuff on it patterned.

Adrian – Now you were forced to use one of my images (meter) a growth "pattern" has taken place (pun intended, I feel dumb for doing it though. hehe!). This reflects the benefits of this collaboration.

FreshFroot

www.freshfroot.com

get it da

freshfroot #2 advertisement created by mike cina
designer, typographer, master of scrapbook mayhem
mike, you shine brighter than most.

1
2
3

mikecina.com
trueistrue.com
weworkforthem.com

4x4: Photoshop and Illustrator – Registration Card

Name ....

Address ....

City .... State/Region ....

Country .... Postcode/Zip ....

E-mail ....

Profession: design student ☐ freelance designer ☐
part of an agency ☐ inhouse designer ☐
other (please specify) ....

Age: Under 20 ☐ 20-25 ☐ 25-30 ☐ 30-40 ☐ over 40 ☐

Do you use: mac ☐ pc ☐ both ☐

How did you hear about this book?
☐ Book review (name) ....
☐ Advertisement (name) ....
☐ Recommendation ....
☐ Catalog ....
☐ Other ....

Where did you buy this book?
☐ Bookstore (name) .... City ....
☐ Computer Store (name) ....
☐ Mail Order ....
☐ Other ....

How did you rate the overall content of this book?
Excellent ☐ Good ☐
Average ☐ Poor ☐

What applications/technologies do you intend to learn in the near future?
....

What did you find most useful about this book?
....

What did you find the least useful about this book?
....

Please add any additional comments
....

What other subjects will you buy a computer book on soon?
....

What is the best computer book you have used this year?
....

Note: This information will only be used to keep you updated about new titles of ED and will not be used for any other purpose or passed to any other third party.

Registration Code : [   ]

For technical support please contact support@friendsofed.com.

Free phone in USA: 800.873.9769
Fax: 312.893.8001

UK Telephone: 0121.258.8858
Fax: 0121.258.8868

Friends of ED writes books for you. Any suggestions, or ideas about how you want information given in your ideal book will be studied by our team. Your comments are always valued at friends of ED.

friendsof
DESIGNER TO DESIGNER™

N.B. If you post the bounce back card below in the UK, please send it to:

friends of ED Ltd.,
30 Lincoln Road, Olton,
Birmingham, B27 6PA, UK.

friendsof

DESIGNER TO DESIGNER™